Remember Me

WOMEN & THEIR FRIENDSHIP QUILTS

Remember Me

Remember me 'tis all I ask
I would not wish for more
Than to be cherished by a heart
So tender and so pure.
I would not ask thee for thy love
Nor blame thee for thy hate
I'll calmly bear the ill of life
And meet the shaft of fate.
But, oh; if sorrow ere should come
To blight thy gay young heart
I then would have thee think of me
That I may share a part
I'm happy when I see the smile
I'm sad to see thee grieve
And I would bare thy every pain
Thy sadness to relieve.
And oh! when friends you value most
Shall meet around thy hearth,
And thy more sober thoughts are lost
In laughter loving mirth,
I then would have thee think of me
That I may share a part
And find a home within thy breast
A home for my young heart

A. E. T.

Remember Me

WOMEN & THEIR FRIENDSHIP QUILTS

Linda Otto Lipsett

THE QUILT DIGEST PRESS

SAN FRANCISCO

Editorial and production direction by Michael M. Kile.
Book design by Jeanne Jambu and Patricia Koren, Kajun Graphics, San Francisco.
Editing assistance by Harold Nadel, San Francisco.
Typographical composition in Cloister by Rock & Jones, Oakland, California.
Calligraphy by Bill Prochnow, San Francisco.
Color photographs not specifically credited were taken by Sharon Risedorph with Lynn Kellner, San Francisco.
Quiltmaking patterns by Laura Nownes.
Printed by Nissha Printing Company, Ltd., Kyoto, Japan.
Color separations by the printer.

"A Piece of Ellen's Dress" appeared originally, in slightly different form,
in *The Quilt Digest 2*, published in 1984.

All vintage photographs and all photographed objects (including quilts)
are the property of the author, unless otherwise noted.

Cover quilt: see page 34.
Cover photograph: Bessie Harris, daughter of Fannie Cord Harris (Chapter VIII).

Fifth printing.

Library of Congress Cataloging in Publication Data

Lipsett, Linda Otto, 1947–
   Remember me.

   Bibliography: p.
   1. Friendship quilts — United States.
2. Quiltmakers — United States — Biography.   I. Title.
NK9112.L57 1985   746.9'7'0922 [B]   85-9525
ISBN 0-913327-04-2
ISBN 0-913327-03-4 (pbk.)

The Quilt Digest Press
955 Fourteenth Street
San Francisco 94114

For my son, Robert

Acknowledgments

For many years the names inscribed on my quilts have led me to wonderful places, from an original Victorian mansion in Vermont to a concrete, hexagonal inn in Wisconsin, from an isolated cemetery in the midst of a vast prairie in Kansas to an historic Congregational church in New Hampshire. Many of those places preserve another time in America, a time when women were making their friendship quilts. They are places to which tourists seldom have reason to go, places far off the main roads; yet, once they were the growing, thriving towns. They had rivers to power gristmills and plenty of wood for log houses.

The people I have met have permanently enriched my life. Their generosity in sharing their information, their helpfulness, their hard work and hospitality have been extraordinary. Surpassing all other rewards, I now have friends and "family" across the country. To all these people (many of them descendants of the people commemorated on my quilts), I wish to say, humbly but emphatically, "Thank you." Without each one of you, some part of this book could not have been written.

Remember Me

Hope Andrews, Langworthy Public Library, Hope Valley, Rhode Island; J. S. Aubrey, Reference Librarian of Newberry Library, Chicago; Carole A. Davey and Thomas E. Frantz, Sheaffer Eaton Textron, Fort Madison, Iowa; Charlotte Rau Ekback; Patricia T. Herr; Charles and Eileen Kelley; Penny McMorris; and Roy Neal.

Betsey! I Wish You a Merry Christmas

Georgia Bumgardner, American Antiquarian Society, Worcester, Massachusetts; Gayle Chandler; Anne Coe, Librarian, and Richard E. Coe, Library Director, Sons of the Revolution Library, Glendale, California; Robert Corrette; Diane Freggiaro, Stockton Historical Society, Stockton, California; Diane Kipper, Putnam Public Library, Putnam, Connecticut; Elaine Lachapelle, President of the Woodstock Historical Society, Woodstock, Connecticut; Erwin and Elsie Neumann; Bill Otto; Tom Parker; Susan Parrish; Michael Pilgrim, National Archives, Washington, D.C.; Mary Roberts; Susan Searchy, Archivist, Sacramento Historical Center, Sacramento, California; and Judy, Samuel, Sam Jr., and Sarah Schumacher.

Till Death Do Us Part

Raymond W. Benson, Pompey Historical Society, Pompey, New York; Roy K. Blowers; Carol and Carl Dennis; Mary Frazee Found; James Frazee; Norma Calkins Harger; Violet A. Hosler and Richard N. Wright, Onondaga Historical Society, Syracuse, New York; Vera Love; Michael Pilgrim, National Archives, Washington, D.C.; and Maxine L. Van Wormer.

Save the Pieces

Mrs. Pascal Covici, Jr.; Barbara Crosby Enright; Diane Friese and Thomas Ladd, Merrimack Public Library, Merrimack, New Hampshire; Elizabeth Fairbairn, Amherst Town Library, Amherst, New Hampshire; Thelma Garstang; Mrs. F. Joyce Gordon; William Rotch, President of the Milford Historical Society, Milford, New Hampshire; Nancy Schooley, Town Clerk, Milford, New Hampshire; Dr. James E. Sefton, Professor of History, California State University, Northridge, California; Mrs. Ida P. Stow; and Mrs. Hazel Whitney, Historical Room of the First Congregational Church, Milford, New Hampshire.

A Piece of Ellen's Dress

Barbara Chiolino; Jane B. Drury; Julia P. Fogg, Chelmsford Historical Society, Chelmsford, Massachusetts; Harold Hanson; James Hanson, Wisconsin State Historical Society, Madison, Wisconsin; Minnie Hanson; Eunice Hoepker; Roderick Kiracofe; Bernard Larson; Julie Lucas, Milton House Museum, Milton, Wisconsin; Polly Mitchell, The Shelburne Museum, Shelburne, Vermont; Walter Otto; George Adams Parkhurst; Susan Parrish; Hazel Petty; Tilmar Roalkvan; and Mr. and Mrs. Dale Turnipseed.

Two Pair Quilting Frames

Mrs. Elizabeth Josephine Evans Brown; Mrs. Franklin Boots; Jane Collins; Ruth E. Daniel; Mr. and Mrs. Don Scarff Evans; Jerry Frost, Friends Historical Library of Swarthmore College, Swarthmore, Pennsylvania; Patricia T. Herr; Ina E. Kelley, Archivist/Curator of the Quaker Collection, Wilmington College, Wilmington, Ohio; Janet Lesher; Sandy Otto; Julie Overton, The Greene County Room, The Greene County District Library, Xenia, Ohio; and Sally Riffle.

Julia's Legacy

Laura Abbott; Bessie Bean; Marilyn Blackwell, Vermont Historical Society, Montpelier, Vermont; Esther Wells Bundy; Robert Corrette; Sally Fisher; Gerald Hall, Town Clerk, Hardwick, Vermont; Cathirene Hay, Trustee, Jeudevine Memorial Library, Hardwick, Vermont; Judith, Tom, Christopher and Timothy Kane; Katharine King, Newbury Library, Newbury, Vermont; Jane C. McKay; Craig Montgomery; Marion Smith Sartelle; Lewis J. Smith; and Ruth Smith.

Fannie's Missing Quilt

Eve Campbell; Nola McGillivray Hampton; Mary Frances McGillivray Hickok; Bernice Kepley; Ray Kepley; Nellie Burr Lattimore; Doug and Barbara McGillivray Lewis; Lucille Lewis; Jim McGillivray; John Ralph McGillivray; Billie Lou Harris Smiley; Dorothy Smiley; Glenna Wiruth; and Jackie Zimmerman.

*I*n addition, I want to thank all those who have accompanied me on research trips: my husband, Robert C. Lipsett; my son, Robert A. Lipsett; my mother, Eileen Kelley; my father, William N. Otto; and my sister-in-law, Sandy Otto, who spent many exhausting hours hand-copying records for me.

Also I would like to thank Penny McMorris and Julie Silber for reading and commenting upon the final text of *Remember Me*.

And, finally, my gratitude to my editor and publisher for consistently adhering to such a high standard of perfection, and for their personal and special care with this book.

Linda Otto Lipsett
Los Angeles
April 1985

*T*his book is the culmination of years of thorough and meticulous research by the author. Linda Otto Lipsett has traveled America, logging thousands of miles, chronicling the lives of the nineteenth-century quiltmakers presented here. Begun as an investigation of her friendship quilt collection, her considerable reading about nineteenth-century American life and customs led her to interview historians, genealogists, government officials and descendants of the quiltmakers. She has dug through stacks of local histories and state and federal government files. Having immersed herself in the historical record, her research ultimately led her onto the quiltmakers' lands and into their homes; she has sat in their kitchens and walked the footpaths they trod. She has read their existing diaries and letters. To the extent that is possible, she has gotten to know the women whose lives she re-creates in this book. Based upon her prodigious research, Linda Otto Lipsett has produced evocative historical narratives that go beyond the dry record of history. As a result, she has written a book that is important not only to quilt aficionados but also to women and men who wish to know more about our female ancestors.

Contents

A block from Betsey Wright's quilt, page 34.

Remember Me

*B*ent
over the family quilting frame, her left hand hidden underneath, the right
one pushing her needle through flowered calico, Leonora Bagley ("A
Piece of Ellen's Dress") found it hard to believe she was making
this quilt for her little sister's wedding and going-away present. Burke, Wisconsin, was fifteen hundred miles away,
a long trip — even if mostly by train — from Ludlow,
Vermont. The thought of separation from her
sister pained Leonora, but Ellen seemed
happy and proud to be going west
where opportunity and riches
abounded. Leonora con-
soled herself that she
and Thomas and
the children
might

someday soon move to Wisconsin too, maybe even next door to Ellen. Whatever Leonora's future, her enthusiasm and excitement over her gift for her sister masked some of her sadness. Her friendship quilt would accompany Ellen to her new home and, if in ink and calico only, a part of Leonora would go with her younger sister.

Seventeen-year-old Lucy Blowers ("Till Death Do Us Part") dared not look back as the horses pulled the wagon up the steep hill, rod by rod away from her beloved home, friends and family in Pompey, New York. Except for baby Elbert Duportal, her mother and father, brother and sister seemed unusually quiet, too. Lucy's tears kept coming as she thought of Grandpa Blowers, Aunt Mary . . . she might never see any of them again. Reassuring herself that it had not been left behind, Lucy's eyes searched the wagon for her trunk. Inside was her friendship quilt; it was especially meaningful to Lucy because she had spent months piecing blocks and collecting signatures from all those she loved and wanted to remember. In her quilt, Lucy had brought a piece of each of their dresses with her, and she could look upon each signed quilt block, as if it were a daguerreotype, seeing her friend's smiling face in her favorite calico. Indeed, Lucy's friendship quilt was a great comfort to her.

In North Woodstock, Connecticut, Betsey M. Wright ("Betsey! I Wish You a Merry Christmas") opened a thick envelope addressed to her. With delight, she gingerly unfolded a beautiful quilt block with the inscription

> Accept this trifle that I send,
> Not as a stranger, but a friend.
> Charlotte N. Follett,
> Hubbardston, Mass., 1847.

What a pretty addition to her collection of blocks for her friendship quilt. At twenty-two, Betsey had no proposal for marriage as yet, nor was she leaving her home; she simply wanted her own friendship quilt. Many of her friends were making them: it was the popular pastime.

*I*ndeed, Betsey Wright, Lucy Blowers and Leonora Bagley, hundreds of miles apart and unknown to one another, were all following a fad that had spread throughout New England as well as along the entire eastern seacoast in the early 1840's. Thousands of friendship quilts were being made. In every little New England village, women were making them. In fact, so many were being made that a woman probably would have her name on at least one, if not several, of these quilts within her lifetime. Certainly any woman, even young girl, could make one. These friendship quilts were of the same simple patterns and techniques as the everyday, scrap-bag quilts that they had each begun learning to make by age four. And, since friendship quilts were put together with pieces of cloth from their scrap bags, they were inexpensive to make. Betsey Wright could make hers attractive without having to buy yards of expensive fine white cotton, chintz or calico. She could make her quilt from remnants and pieces of clothing, used or new, and from blocks, already pieced, given to her by family and friends.

For these reasons, the friendship quilt was steadily moving west over the Appalachians and Alleghenies, over the Wilderness Road and the National Road, into states such as Ohio and Michigan, Wisconsin and Kansas, by wagon, stage, train, canal boat and steamboat. And, although patterns, fabrics and inked inscriptions varied from one region to another, America's friendship quilts are remarkably similar to each other.

Most importantly, they all are made up of a one-block pattern repeated throughout the entire quilt. That pattern was usually pieced, but appliqué or a combination of appliqué and piecing techniques was sometimes used. And many, or all, of the blocks in a quilt have names on them, either inscribed in ink or embroidered in silk thread or cotton floss.

*S*igning one's name to cloth was not an innovative idea around 1840, when women began inscribing their first friendship quilts. As part of their schooling, they had most likely spent many hours learning to count threads and to write the alphabet and numbers in fine cross-stitching for their samplers. This ability to make cross-stitched letters was a valuable tool. Following the customs of their mothers, grandmothers and great-grandmothers, they had carefully cross-stitched their initials and a number into homespun, hand-woven sheets, pillowcases and towels for their hope chests. It was only practical that they should do this: the items would be rotated in use for equal wear; also, the owner could identify easily her own linens in large family washings. Women even cross-stitched their initials or names in home-dyed yarns onto homespun or hand-woven woolen blankets, or with fine silk or cotton thread into a special place on their quilts. Indeed, these women and girls were adding their names to their belongings decades before the 1840's. But, generally, they were adding their names only in careful, time-consuming stitches. It was not until the 1830's that they began using ink in place of thread to mark their quilts.

For centuries, there had been recipes and preparations for indel-

Nine Patch variation quilt top, by Louisa Atwood, Carpenter's Landing, New Jersey,
1842–1847, 84 1/2 × 86 1/2 inches, pieced cottons and cotton chintzes.

ible ink; yet, "whereas soot or ivory black was the chief ingredient in that of the ancients," in the first half of the nineteenth century, "gall-nuts, copperas and gum" made up both sold and homemade inks.[1] This new ink was a "muddy fluid" and had "minute particles of . . . iron and tannin"[2] in it that caused cloth to rot quickly, leaving only a ghostly silhouette of the inked in-

Early, deteriorating ink signature.

scriptions, as well as giving those inks brown and yellow tints, instead of good blacks. Beginning in the mid-1830's, however, there was a

transition to "modern inks." Patents were filed in France for new "indelible writing ink" without iron: one formula was of silver nitrate, ammonia and lampblack, another of silver nitrate, gum arabic, water and lampblack.[3] America followed with a patent filed July 16, 1841, by Thomas J. Spear of New Orleans, for "improvement in the manufacture of indelible writing-ink."[4]

These new indelible inks, "chiefly composed of nitrate of silver preparations," were "found best adapted for marking linen."[5] Thus, by the early 1840's, women could at last begin using ink with confidence that their valuable articles would not be damaged.

Besides new inks, there was also a dramatic change in pen styles, from the "gray goose quill" to "a good steel pen."[6] And there existed fervent arguments for both types. "A good steel pen lasts longer than a quill, and when it is past service, you have only to throw it away and fit in another to the holder."[7] "Prejudice, however, was strong against them, and up to 1835 or thereabouts quills maintained their full sway, and much later among the old-fashioned folks."[8] Many people preferred "their elasticity,"[9] as compared with the more inflexible steel pens. As a compromise, the new nibs of steel and gold were often used with the quill pens.

*F*or the first time, in all parts of settled America, from their clapboards in New England to their log houses in the Midwest or wherever their husbands had transported them, women were in touch with fashion and the latest trends because of widely circulated magazines, the most popular being *The Lady's Book* of the early 1830's, later known as *Godey's Lady's Book and Magazine,* edited by a New England woman, Sarah Josepha Hale. In 1840, *Godey's* boasted a circulation of 17,500; just prior to the Civil War, circulation had reached 150,000.[10] But, in fact, many more women saw these monthly magazines, for each magazine was collected and saved, read, re-read, then circulated among friends for years. The magazines were important to the eastern women of the cities and towns who dressed in the

latest fashions from abroad and to the pioneer women, as their best link to the society they had left. A woman in an isolated valley on the new frontier might own or have the opportunity to read a *Godey's* printed many months, even years, earlier; yet, it was still her best link with fashion.

In addition to fashion plates and instructions for embroidery and

other needlework, *Godey's* printed poems, fiction, music, receipts and household hints. In the 1830's, friendship was romanticized and personified in verses entitled "Friendship," "Friendship's Altar" and "Remember Me" ("There are not two other words in the language that can recall a more fruitful train of past remembrances of friendship than these.").[11] Among the newly composed music published in the magazine was "I'll Remember Thee."

One way of concretely demonstrating friendship was the autograph album. It was in existence many years prior to the emergence of the friendship quilt, as indicated by *Godey's* in March of 1835, in lines entitled "Remember Me": "Have you an ancient album, the repository of mementoes of early affection? Turn over its leaves, stained by the finger of time — sit down and ponder upon the names enrolled on them — each speaks, each says Remember me."[11] In 1830, the first year of *The Lady's*

Book, there were occasional lines and verses with references to "the Album." In "Tribute to an Album," a woman is awakened in the night, "But my sister pale, with a gray-goose quill, And an ALBUM — sight of sorrow! 'Get up!' she cried, 'and a long page fill, For this book must go back to-morrow!' "[12] In the issue for January, 1832, "Friendship's Offering" was printed: "And ere the book I send, On *that* leaf I will trace the name Of *my own dearest* Friend."[13] Two years later, in August, 1834, appeared the story "by Miss Leslie," entitled "The Album — A Sketch," of a fashionable couple at West Point: "And do you steadily persist in refusing to write in my album?" "I have foresworn albums," replied Sunderland, "... the gods have not made me poetical.... Nothing is more contemptible than mediocre poetry."[14] There appear to be no articles with "album" in their titles again until April, 1838. Then, the word "album" appears more frequently: "Lines written in an Album" ("Here friendship's soft hand is entwining"),[15] "Dedication for an Album" and "Lines written in the

Remember me
Horace P Worden
West Halifax
Vermont

Page from an autograph album.

Album of a Little Stranger." In April, 1839, "For an Album" was "Written for the Lady's Book":

Write for your Album! well I may —
To please you is a virtuous aim;
Yet, you will frown on such a lay
As I, unaided, know to frame.[16]

The autograph album was now popular in America, and Sarah J.

Hale, an astute editor, quickly began incorporating its popularity into her monthly magazines, with "Dedicatory Lines for an Album" written by a woman in New Hampshire: "And such may this fair Album be, A casket of the brightest gems; Sweet blossoms from affection's tree, Pearls set in Friendship's diadems."[17] In each monthly magazine there were new ones: "Lines to My Sister," "Lines from a Lady's Album." In April, 1841 appeared an article entitled "An Evening's Conversation About Autographs":

"How many curious devices there have been for perpetuating the names of distinguished persons," said the Schoolmaster, as he carefully turned over the leaves of Ellen Marvin's Book of Autographs. "This paper-and-ink system seems a very fragile hold on immortality here below; and yet it may prove more enduring than the plates of brass and pillars of marble so ostentatiously set up in the olden times."[18]

So it was that the cycle had come full circle and the album of a decade earlier was a fad once again, but now for the first time, with the help of magazines, young women could copy sophisticated, supposedly newly composed lines into their friends' books.

It was by this time that women began writing these verses, and others, with their new inks onto cloth pages — the pieced and appliquéd blocks of their quilts. And at this time in the early 1840's, two separate, very different types of quilts emerged: the scrap-bag, repeated-block friendship quilt of this book, and the more formal album quilt with many, often appliquéd, patterns. The simple friendship quilt, anyone could make; the album quilt required money for large quantities of cloth and skill and leisure time to appliqué and piece the difficult curved seams. Their only shared characteristic is that all friendship quilts and some

A block from Betsey Wright's quilt, page 34, displaying a verse typical of those found in Godey's.

album quilts have names inscribed or embroidered on them; their purposes were, at times, similar. Yet, over the years, the terms "friendship quilt" and "album quilt" have been used interchangeably, and mistakenly, to group these quilts into the same simple, confused category. Until now, the friendship quilt has been misplaced, even overlooked; it should not be.

*F*rom 1840 to 1875, friendship quilts were made in staggering numbers by a broad cross section of American women, and it was in the 1840's and 1850's that the style reached its zenith. During the 1840's, the inscriptions on the quilt blocks were, often, imitations spirited off from magazines and the popular autograph albums of the day. An example is Betsey Wright's

quilt with long verses, some of which are similar to lines appearing in *Godey's* monthly issues. But by the mid-1850's and 1860's, women began writing shorter inscriptions. Many times they inscribed names only; at other times, they listed names, locations, dates. These later friendship quilts embodied the same

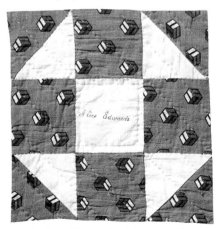

A Shoo Fly block, with name only, from the quilt on page 30.

strong sentiments penned onto earlier ones, but the detail, quality and formality of the inscriptions gradually declined. In these ways, friendship quilts mirror the changes occurring throughout American quiltmaking at this time. By the 1870's, the nation, and particularly the North, was more prosperous after the hard times of the Civil War decade. During the war, many women had been forced back to their spinning wheels, looms and dye pots in order for their families

There was a new needlework fad that was sweeping the towns and cities, even reaching into the rural areas of America. By 1876, the crazy quilt was coming into vogue. Quilt style and fabrics were changing. Cottons in quilts were "considered hopelessly old-fashioned."[19] Godey's had begun conveying that message to women at least twenty years earlier: "Patchwork quilts, unless in silks, are rarely seen in cities, the glory of our grandmothers having passed away."[20]

Rail Fence, *by Sarah S. Evans, Greene County, Ohio, c. 1880–1900, 60 × 71 inches, pieced silks, typical of late-nineteenth-century silk patchwork, following the fashion of the time. Sarah S.'s earlier friendship quilt is on page 92.*

Mid-nineteenth-century fabric-stamping kit, found in Montgomery County, Pennsylvania. Collection of Dr. and Mrs. Donald M. Herr.

to survive, but with better times, and the industrial age, women could supplement their bedding with factory-made blankets. They could even order these bedcoverings by mail from E. C. Allen or Montgomery Ward. Women continued to make patchwork quilts in large numbers but, by the mid-1870's, there was a definite decline in the popularity of friendship quilts.

And by the mid-1870's, with millions of dollars' worth of silk being produced in the United States alone, women had the means to follow the dictates of the new fashion. Soon they could even order pre-cut squares of "silks for patchwork."[21] Instead of a friendship quilt or cotton appliquéd quilt, they made silk and velvet crazy quilts with "an allover focus, rather than an emphasis on individual blocks."[22]

Certainly these crazy quilts were unlike any of their friendship quilts; yet, in many examples, the quiltmaker put her initials or name, and those of family members or friends, onto her crazy quilt, maintaining a small part of a deeply implanted tradition.

*T*he friendship quilt was the product of one or many makers. Leonora Bagley had pieced each of the blocks for her sister's quilt herself. She made each block out of two scraps of co-ordinating cottons: dresses or shirts of the person whose name was to be signed on the block. Then Leonora asked someone with excellent penmanship and experience in writing on cloth to inscribe every block. After assembling the blocks into the top, she, along with several family members, quilted it.

When all the blocks were to be signed by one hand, as on Leonora's quilt, it was a common practice to baste a small strip of paper with the intended person's name to each block, so that no one would

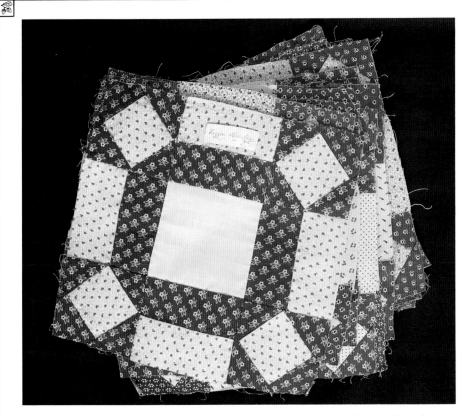

later, Leonora Bagley made her sister's quilt in Ludlow, Vermont. Leonora did not make hers for a poster bed, and she chose white for the sashing; otherwise, these two quilts are alike.

Also, friendship quilts made within a certain area, within the same period, often share many of the same characteristics, including pattern blocks, sashings between blocks, quilt backs, quilting thread and inscriptions. And many friendship quilts share similar quilting patterns. Two from Vermont illustrate this: Leonora Bagley quilted a winding vine with leaves in the sashing of her sister's quilt and Julia Stevens Crosby ("Julia's Legacy") stitched a wreath of leaves and cherries into the plain blocks of her quilt.

be accidentally omitted. Many times these names were cut from signatures on letters, to be sure of the spelling.

But a quiltmaker might prefer her family members' and friends' own signatures on her friendship quilt. She could cut white (or unbleached) muslin, homespun linen, fine-grade cotton or, in rare instances, silk into the correct template size for a block and easily put the small piece of cloth into an envelope and send it to her loved one to be signed, then returned. Later, her scrap bag hanging from her chair, she chose printed cottons and solids to be used with the precious signed piece for the completed block. On the other hand, if she preferred, she could easily mail or give a quilt pattern to her friend or family member who, she hoped, would piece the requested block from remnants of her dresses, her husband's shirts or her children's frocks, sign the center piece and return the completed keepsake.

Indeed, with so many choices available for making friendship

quilts, it is remarkable that the results were so similar. In fact, many quilts from diverse areas are almost identical. The Crosby family ("Save the Pieces") made their quilt in 1849, in Milford, New Hampshire; many miles northwest, and five years

*I*t is true that, with time, certain standard patterns for the friendship quilt emerged. The *Chimney Sweep* and *Album Patch* seem to have been the favorites and, from examples surviving today, the ma-

Friendship blocks, with names basted to them, ready for inscribing.

21

Unknown pattern, made by a member of the John D. Langworthy family,
Hopkinton, Rhode Island, c. 1865–1875, 94 × 94 ½ inches, pieced cottons.

jority made. Lucy Blowers chose the *Chimney Sweep* for her New York friendship quilt in 1848; Fannie Cord Harris ("Fannie's Missing Quilt") used the same pattern decades later, in 1891, halfway across the country in Golden, Kansas. Regardless of the trends, however, the quiltmaker was never confined to certain patterns: she could

Detail of backing.

choose her pattern from any that had a patch to sign, and sometimes, like the maker of the Langworthy quilt (this page), simply pieced (or appliquéd) a small cross, strip or square to the center of an otherwise inappropriate pattern block for the inscription. The only rule she most often followed was that plain fabric be used for the inscriptions. Otherwise, the maker created friendship quilts from nearly every popular pattern of her day: stars, *Nine Patch* and its many variations, *Double Pyramid, Log Cabin, Mariner's Compass, Basket,* to name but a few.

She also used several means to inscribe her blocks. She could use ink, in longhand, block letters or

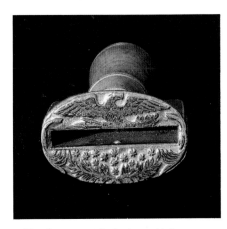

Hand stamp, with slot into which a name plate could be inserted, used to decorate friendship-quilt blocks.

S. J. Simonds

Hand-stenciled signature, from the Basket *quilt on page 29.*

printed with hand stamps. And, as was popular in the 1840's around the Maryland-Pennsylvania-New Jersey area, she could hide her name within elaborate, delicate, tiny ink drawings of objects such as leaves, urns, flowers, birds or fountains.

Clarenda . Sanford

Cross-stitched signature.

From the 1840's to 1860's, she may have chosen to cross-stitch her name or initials onto her friendship quilt blocks but, by 1875, names were usually embroidered in running, outline, or backstitches, with many strands of embroidery floss.

Mrs. Saralla. Bland

Running-stitch signature.

No longer did she wish to sign her name in the earlier, delicate fashion, with quill pen or fine, minuscule cross-stitch. Her signature, a statement of herself, of her growing independence and self-worth, had changed: it was now larger, bolder.

*V*irtually every quiltmaker had rules governing how her friendship quilt would be signed. And, in many cases, such guidelines may have been learned from needlewomen in her family or community. Leonora, in Vermont, listed all children and unmarried young adults with first and last names, whereas she gave the respectful title of "Mr." or "Mrs." to married persons. Isabel Moore Crosby, however, when organizing her family friendship quilt in Milford, New

Embroidery-floss signatures with date.

Hampshire, decided that a person's full name, without a title and including middle initials of the maiden name, would be used to inscribe a block. And Lucy Blowers of New York identified her family members by relationship, like "Aunt Mary Jane Blowers" and "My little Brother Elbert Duportal," but friends on her quilt all have the title of "Miss" or "Mrs." Unfortunately, there were some quiltmakers who decided first initials with last names, or even first and

S. M. I.

Initials, from the quilt on page 28.

last initials, should be used, making their quilts impossible to document conclusively, if at all.

The quiltmaker usually included a block of her own somewhere on the quilt, but many times she used only initials for part or all of her name. An example is Isabel Moore

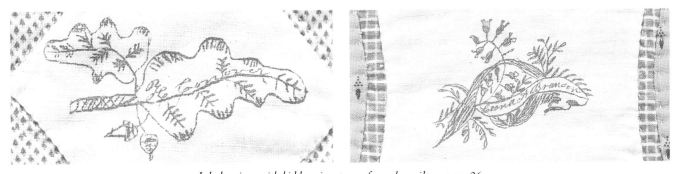

Ink drawings with hidden signatures, from the quilt on page 26.

Block with name, place and date.

Block with child's age.

Crosby, who modestly wrote "Save the Pieces. I.M. Crosby." In other cases, a maker might sign her name to more than one block, as did Sarah S. Evans ("Two Pair Quilting Frames") in Greene County, Ohio.

Lucy Blowers, like many other friendship-quilt makers, did not include any men on her quilt, only three small boys. These were quilts made by women, for women and, in some cases, totally excluding men.

Besides names, the quiltmaker might choose to include other information, such as the town or township, county, state or date. Especially on friendship quilts of the 1840's and 1850's, loving messages and verses — either Biblical or secular — were written by the different quilt-block signers. Onto the friendship quilt made for circuit rider David D. Graves in 1842 in New Jersey, Elsworth Holeman penned, "How beautiful are the feet of them that preach the Gospel of peace and bring glad tidings of good things." In Ascutneyville, Vermont, in 1853, Susan Tenney wrote "To Mrs. M—, 'Remember all who love Thee, And all who are loved by Thee.'" Almost every block of Betsey Wright's quilt has wonderful, long verses from her loved ones, such as:

> Accept my friend this little pledge
> Your love and friendship to engage
> If ere we should be called to part
> Let this be settled in your heart
> That when this little peace you see
> You ever will remember me
> M.E.A.
> Woodstock
> 1847.

Besides verses, sometimes more personal information was written, such as a child's or elderly person's age. And, sadly, sometimes a mother would record the death of a child, as did Hannah Cranmer in 1843 in Cranmertown, New Jersey. She wrote, "Isaiah Cranmer Born

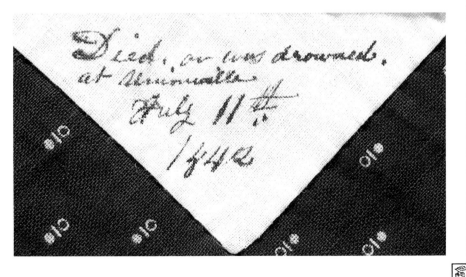

representations of these women's quilting skills.

Of course, there are friendship quilts as finely and heavily quilted as any "best" appliquéd or pieced quilts. Kansan Fannie Cord Harris marked the plain blocks of her quilt top with a graceful feather template, and then quilted the three layers with tiny, straight stitches. This was *her* best quilt, and she wanted to do her finest work on it.

But Fannie Cord Harris, like Leonora Bagley and Betsey Wright Lee, had no intention of her quilt ever being used. The friendship quilt went hand in hand with the autograph albums popular at the time: it was a treasured keepsake. And especially when given as a going-away present, a quilt upon which towns were inscribed served as a nineteenth-century directory. With her friendship quilt, a woman would carry all the information she needed in order to write to any of her friends and family back home. It was even better than an address book, because it was large and difficult to misplace. And she could use her friendship quilt to decorate her sparsely furnished frontier cabin or drab dugout on the prairie.

It is because friendship quilts were treasured and seldom used by their owners that they have survived today, many of them in excellent condition. Indeed, the nine-

February 12th 1816, Died April 15th 1816." And, on the same quilt top, young Louisa Atwood, the quiltmaker, penned in remembrance of her little boy, "Died, or was drowned. at Unionville July 11th 1842." What *had* been his fate? She did not know. Julia Stevens Crosby in Vermont, however, did not wish to record death on *her* quilt, even though she did include blocks for deceased family members. On the contrary, she wrote dates of birth.

*U*nlike her "best" red-and-green, floral appliquéd quilts of the same period, large amounts of fine quilting were not so important on a quiltmaker's friendship quilt. In this respect, the quilting is similar to that seen on her other scrap-bag quilts; however, in many examples, there is even less quilting on her friendship quilt than on these every-day bedcoverings: the quiltmaker

need quilt it only enough to hold the layers together. She was making her friendship quilt primarily for its sentimental value, not for use. Betsey Wright Lee in Connecticut certainly believed this as she hurriedly quilted hers, as did the women quilting their gorgeous *Full-blown Tulip* top for Reverend David D. Graves in New Jersey. Surely these quilts were not fair

Full-blown Tulip, *made for Methodist Episcopal circuit rider David D. Graves*
by the women of several Methodist Episcopal churches of Burlington, Monmouth and Ocean Counties, New Jersey,
1842–1843, 101 × 101½ inches, pieced and appliquéd cottons.

teenth-century quiltmaker's "best" quilts have also survived (many in as fine condition). But what sets the friendship quilt apart and makes it important to us today, besides the inscriptions, is that it is closely related in style and feeling to everyday, scrap-bag quilts with their wonderful variety of fabrics. Like the homespun or calico dress, simple country quilts were *used*: tugged and pulled at, washed in kettles of boiling water with homemade lye soap, bleached by the sun, all the while being patched and darned so they would last another year. With her new baby arriving soon and a houseful of children already, a nine-teenth-century woman needed all the quilts she had, and she used them until they were fit only to be used as batting within a replacement quilt.

Her friendship quilt was different. It had names on it, names of her loved ones, some of them no longer living, and it held memories.

That made it special. It was her personal treasure, and she stored it in her old hope chest or some other special place. (Fannie Cord Harris put hers inside a cardboard box with her name and "Golden, Kansas" penciled on the outside.) After all, she deserved something nice, something that was just hers, something that softened some of her daily struggle and relentless toil.

*T*he lives of the women in this book are all different, yet they are all shaped by birth, death, religion and war. Many of the women, like Sarah S. Evans on her farm in Ohio, Betsey Wright Lee in a clapboard house in Connecticut and Fannie Cord Harris in her rock house in Kansas, were strong — survivors despite their tragedies and hardships. Others, like twenty-two-year-old Ellen Spaulding Reed in the Wisconsin wilderness and thirty-eight-year-old Lucy Blowers Tol-

Double Pyramid, c. 1860, origin unknown, 83 × 82 inches, pieced cottons, one of a pair.

Mariner's Compass, 1853, Ascutneyville, Vermont,
85 × 87 inches, pieced and appliquéd cottons.

ford, died young, of disease and loneliness.

The bearing and raising of children was most often the nineteenth-century woman's greatest responsibility. Many of the women had numerous babies: Sarah Evans in Ohio gave birth to fifteen; her daughter-in-law Sarah S. Evans, to nine; Betsey Wright Lee, to nine. But then there were some, like Ellen Spaulding Reed, who could not have any. To save face, she wrote, "Babies are as thick out here as flies in the sumer, but poor folks like us cannot afford it."[23]

And the War Between the States affected all their lives and joined women together. They had sons, husbands, brothers and fathers fighting: Sarah S. Evans in Ohio, Lucy Blowers Tolford in Michigan, Betsey Wright Lee in Connecticut, along with thousands and thousands of mothers and wives all over the

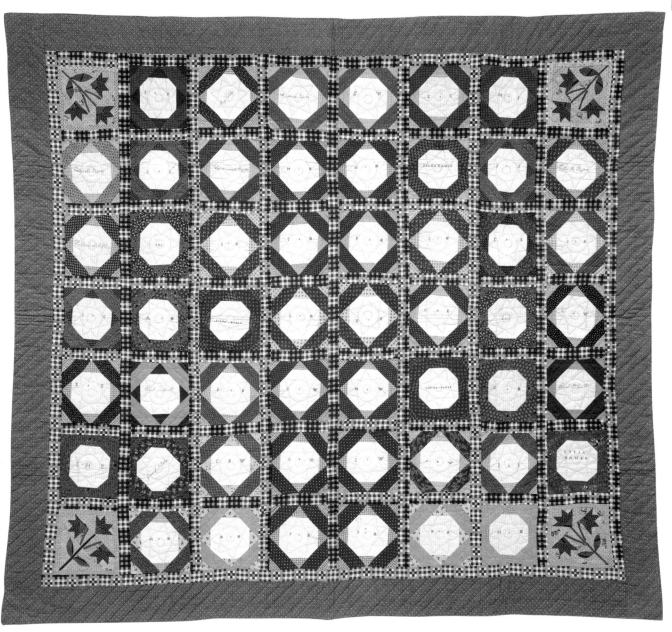

Unknown pattern, c. 1850-1870, Lancaster County,
Pennsylvania, 92 × 82 inches, pieced and appliquéd cottons.

North and the South, each fervently prayed that the brutal war would soon be over. Tragically, many of their loved ones did not survive. Across America, women mourned—Lucy Blowers Tolford for her Henry, Sarah S. Evans for her son, Betsey Wright Lee for her husband. Death: it pervaded their lives, especially with so many of their children dying young. Then the horrors of war had taken more.

But nineteenth-century American women fought to survive. They had strength and steadfastness from their hearty, persistent Puritan and pioneer ancestors, and strong religious faiths, whether they were Quakers, Baptists, Methodists or Congregationalists. Sometimes, though, it was the seemingly small things in their lives, the creative things like their friendship quilts, that cheered them so that they could go on.

Fannie Cord Harris, Ellen Spaulding Reed, Betsey Wright Lee, Sarah S. Evans—each treasured her quilt because of its inscriptions. Today, their quilts are still important for that reason, but not as cloth autograph albums. Now they are living records, evidence that these women existed. In many instances, friendship quilts are the *only* remaining records of the women whose names are inscribed on them.

This is particularly true of quilts made prior to 1850. Only the names of "heads of families" were listed on government census records be-

Basket, c. 1840–1860, found in Ohio, 88 × 88 inches, pieced and appliquéd cottons, cut for a poster bed.

Chimney Sweep in a Garden Maze, c. 1840–1860, New England, 85 × 85 inches, pieced cottons.

fore this date. A woman's name was listed on the census only if she herself were the head of the household, generally due to the death of her husband. A region's vital records for a certain period of time may not exist, due to storage problems, fires or floods, or simply because they were not kept, as in the case of the State of New York, which did not record births and deaths until 1880. Genealogies and county and town histories, written usually in great detail, listing persons living in that place during the time of publication or in the recent past, rarely mention a man's wife. Only *his* successes and virtues are lauded. It is often only in the family Bible that a woman's name was recorded, but that usually was passed

Shoo Fly, *by Sarah Eaton, Coxsackie, New York, c. 1865–1875, 79 × 76 inches, pieced cottons.*

down to descendants, and is often difficult, if not impossible, to locate, if it does indeed still exist.

Generally, the most lasting record of a woman's existence is her gravestone, but even that may have been worn by storms and time and vandalism until her name is erased, or the stone fallen and slowly buried, removed or lost. With that stone, any record of her existence is forever gone.

It was not woman's desire, however, to be forgotten. And in one simple, unpretentious way, she created a medium that would outlive even many of her husband's houses, barns and fences: she signed her name in friendship onto cloth and, in her own way, cried out,
        "Remember me."

Six-pointed Star, *1868–1872, Vermont, 78 × 87 inches, pieced and appliquéd cottons.*

Nine Patch *variation, c. 1840–1850, Connecticut, 87 × 88 inches, pieced cottons, cotton chintzes and silks.*

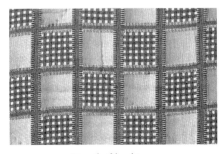

Detail of backing.

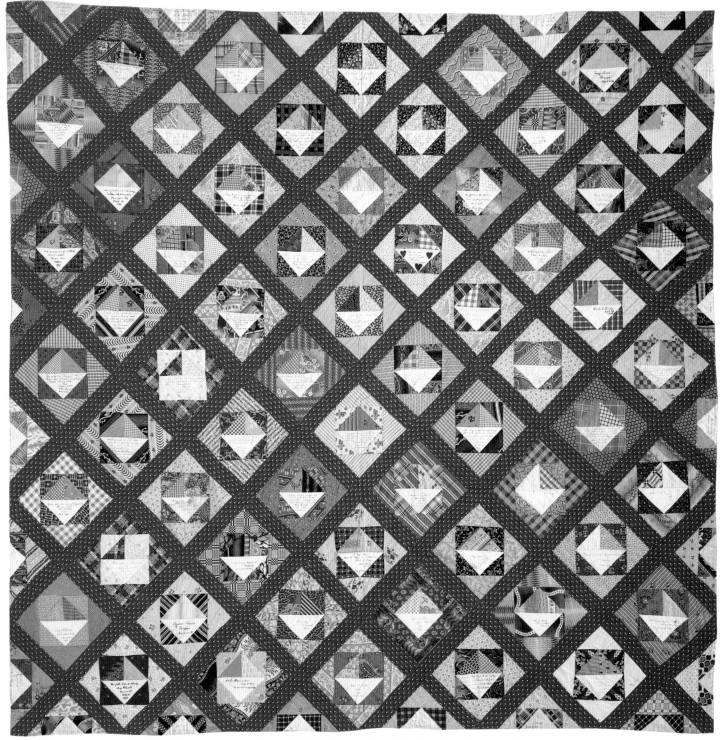

*Unknown pattern, by Betsey M. Wright Lee, North Woodstock and Putnam, Connecticut,
blocks pieced between 1846 and 1851, quilted c. 1875, 88 × 87 inches, pieced cottons.*

Betsey! I Wish You a Merry Christmas

Along-
side the narrow,
winding road of North
Woodstock, Connecticut,
several cows and scraggly
sheep peacefully graze on the
rock-embedded hillsides near
early clapboard and brick houses.
A sparkling brook meanders
through. Across the road is forest.
In the summer, all is hidden in
those dense woods, but in the late
fall, the forest floor is exposed, covered
only in a soft, damp, rust-colored carpet.
It might seem that these tall forests have always

been here, that they have stood for hundreds of years as they do today. Yet within them is an undeniable presence of the past. Parallel to the road, and slicing across the forest at right angles for as far as the eye can see, are rocks and boulders, large and small, round and split, all neatly fitted together; these are fences of another time, marking off a farmer's plowed and planted fields, keeping in his livestock, saying "this is mine"—borders so indomitable that they have remained, some for over two hundred years, an unyielding, integral part of the land, the forest having grown up again around them.

It was only yesterday, a blink of the eye in the space of time, that this land was cleared, plowed up and planted in wheat and corn, the brook splashing over the rocks and providing power to the gristmill in the busy neighboring village of East Woodstock, with its tannery, general store, sawmill, smithy, carriage shop, and the Congregational Church beside the commons.

*B*etsey was twenty-three, and this Woodstock area was her world. It was Christmas 1846, a joyous time in Betsey's life, a time when her mother and father, brothers and sister had all been together. And her seventeen-year-old brother Phineas had given her a humble, yet most significant, gift: a simple, pieced patchwork block with the handwritten greeting "Betey! I wish you a merry christmas Phineas G Wright North Woodstock CT Dec 25 1846." That little block was among the beginnings of an heirloom, for in September of that year Betsey had begun collecting friendship blocks with meaningful messages from her family and friends.

It was difficult for Betsey to watch her friends, one by one, get-

Early view of East Woodstock, Connecticut.
Photograph courtesy of Charles H. Cady.

many months' journey and gotten as far as Stockton, California, before dying on October 6, 1849. No gold, no riches, no husband, all at once. The family was in shock. The quilt block her father had signed for Betsey nearly three years earlier was now one of her only mementos of him. Ironically, it was signed "When troubles assail you flee to the Bible. from f̲a̲t̲h̲e̲r̲ Phineas Wright East Woodstock Conn—."

After their wedding, Betsey and Abner made their home with Betsey's recently widowed mother, brothers Ebenezer and Phineas and sister Sarah. Five-foot-ten Abner worked daily as a farrier at the blacksmith shop in North Woodstock while Betsey kept house, sewed and knitted, always with thoughts of her exciting future in mind. And Betsey thought of children, Abner's and her children.

ting married, she being twenty-three and with no proposal in sight. Her friend Lucretia M. Dean was the new bride of Reverend Gore, of Illinois. Before her marriage, she had signed a block for Betsey "Love wisdom, love virtue, love God and be happy." And Sally B. Chandler, married over one year now, had signed, "Jesus answered, my kingdom is not of this world." Lucy B. Lillie was married six years already. She wrote, "When far a way from this dear spot, In a distant land do thou in [First?] pray, and when it is Weill with you, remember me."

Betsey continued to collect blocks for her friendship quilt for over three years, until her marriage to the blacksmith from Vermont, Abner Lee, on January 17, 1850. Betsey was twenty-six; dark-haired and brown-eyed Abner was only twenty-two. Long had she waited for this moment in her life, when she should be so happy. Her happiness, however, was diminished by the deeply felt absence of her father, Phineas. The past spring, he had been one of the first New Englanders to go west to California. It seemed the depression would continue forever. He had sincerely believed he could work for a while finding gold in California and be

able to provide a better life for his family. But it was only recently that Betsey's mother had received word of her husband's death. Phineas had never reached the gold fields. He had arrived in San Francisco after

After waiting so many years to begin her family, Betsey soon began catching up with her married friends' families, with a baby nearly every year. On August 20, 1851, a little girl was born to Betsey. They named her Sarah I. J. after Betsey's mother and sister and called her Belle to avoid confusion.[1] While still nursing Belle, Betsey discovered she was pregnant again and, in 1852, gave birth to another little girl, Bessie. A little over one year later, on September 8, 1853, their first son, Phineas W., entered the world. Betsey's life was fuller, richer now than it had ever been before.

Not yet married four years, Betsey and Abner had three children and needed a home of their own. They soon moved to Thompson, a small neighboring village. Their property was on the side road directly off the commons, with a stone

Betsey and Abner's home in Thompson, Connecticut.

wall surrounding it and a wooden gate opening to a small clapboard two-story house on a hill overlooking woods. It was a pleasant house, and Betsey was happy here, even though she was exhausted most of the time. She was pregnant again; not long after their move, with baby

Susanna's arrival in April of 1855, there were four small ones in the Lee household in Thompson.

But, in July of 1857, there was sadness for Betsey when her younger sister, Sarah, only twenty-two and living in Putnam, to which she had moved with their mother, died of typhoid. Three more of Betsey's friendship quilt blocks — those her sister had signed more than ten years earlier — were now numbered among Betsey's most precious keepsakes. Two of them said simply "Sisters offering," the third one "Love God & be happy Woodstock, Conn. Oct. 23, 18.46." Sarah and Betsey had been close, and Sarah had loved the children and always been near enough to help Betsey if necessary. Betsey missed her sister.

In the years following her sister's death, Betsey bore two more girls, Eva in 1858 and Lelia on August 21, 1859. By the time Abner and Betsey had been married ten years, there were already five darling, giggling, petite girls, aged five months to nine years, and one little boy, aged six.

❧

Let no dark cloud of trouble rise,
With frowning brow severe,
To shroud in gloom thy sumry skies,
And cause a flowing tear.
　　　Huldah F. May

Indeed, as if a dark cloud came over them, Betsey's wearisome yet gratifying days changed abruptly. First, eight-year-old Bessie became ill. Betsey, herself five months pregnant, made desperate attempts to save her little girl, but to no avail; Bessie died on October 11, 1860, and Abner had their daughter's simple stone engraved:

Weep not Mother for your Bessie,
For her troubles they are over
Though she sleeps tis but in Jesus
Prepare to greet her in a better place.

Betsey was still grieving over the loss of her little Bessie when, only four months after her daughter's funeral, Betsey gave birth to twin boys—boys that Abner and Betsey had been hoping for—but, tragically, they were born too tiny, too weak: one died three days later, the other at twenty-two days. Betsey was weakened from childbirth and numb with sadness and despair, but there was no mercy for her. Two months later, on May 20, 1861, smiling, innocent Eva was also taken from her and buried beside her brothers and sister.

Betsey agonized over the losses of her precious children. She cried out for answers, for comfort and help. Why did they have to suffer so? How could she go on? How could she, amidst debilitating grief, even function, let alone care for her other four? Would they be taken away from her, too? But, after so many tears, after so much hurt and pain, Betsey was with child again; Hattie was born in April 1863.

There was another "dark cloud of trouble" that had loomed overhead for the past two years. Betsey and Abner had feared daily that Abner would have to go off to war. At thirty-five, Abner had avoided the army as long as he could, but on March 3, 1863, Congress had passed a national draft law including "all able-bodied male citizens between twenty and forty-five."[2] Betsey had been expecting a baby any day at that time, and Abner had delayed enlisting until the last possible moment. He did not want to leave Betsey alone in Thompson with a tiny baby and four children, the eldest, Sarah, only eleven, but he had no choice, now that the war was intensifying.

On Monday, December 14, 1863, Betsey resignedly kissed Abner good-bye and sadly watched him close the gate. That bleak, wintry morning, Abner was headed forty miles south to Norwich, Connecti-cut, and then wherever the army might send him.

A sinking, sick feeling came over Betsey as she closed the door. Abner had gone off to his blacksmith shop daily except on Sunday for years; yet he had always returned in the evening. For fourteen years they had been together. Betsey's loneliness overwhelmed her. And winter was setting in: how could she endure without her husband? A desperate feeling came over her. She had no way of knowing where he would be sent, and it would be many days, maybe even several weeks, before his first letter could get to her. Yet she could not weaken; she had little ones who needed her. All she could do was pray, pray for Abner.

*C*hristmas was grim that year; it was only eleven days earlier that Abner had tenderly embraced her that last time, although for Betsey it seemed an eternity. Abner was constantly on her mind. She worried that he was out in the snow and fierce winds without enough warm clothes, without good food. And she longed for a letter. Now Betsey's happiness centered upon letters from her husband. She was relieved when Abner wrote that he was well, in Company F of the First Regiment of the Connecticut Cavalry, and was one of the blacksmiths for his regiment. It appeared that Abner would not be just another of thousands in the bloody battles. He was too valuable. He was a blacksmith. The Union needed *him*. And, whenever he was paid, Abner sent money so that his wife and children could live, if not comfortably, at least with the essentials.[3]

The snows had melted, leaves were beginning to appear on the trees, grass and wild flowers were sprouting. There was new life all around, and a renewed spirit of hope. Betsey had learned to adjust to conversations in pen and ink. Abner was fine, even enjoying his job as a blacksmith. Their letters continued until July. Then none. At first, Betsey assured herself the next letter would come; it was only late. Maybe it was lost. But she could not suppress her fear that something had happened.

Betsey was beside herself with worry, when a letter finally came from a friend of Abner's in the regiment: Abner was captured at Reams Station, Virginia, on July 1, 1864. That was all he knew. Abner himself desperately tried to get word to Betsey that he was at Andersonville Prison, in Georgia.[4] Now, Betsey suffered with the knowledge that Abner was a prisoner of war. The newspapers and rumors abounded with stories of dehumanizing Southern prisons, the most notorious being Andersonville. Everyone had heard of the horrors there. There was "no shelter whatever"[5] from thunderstorms, cold or severe heat; hundreds were dying weekly of scurvy and starvation, with the scant rations of "a pint and a half of coarse corn-meal and half a teaspoonful of salt daily," some periods of "two and three days at a time without a morsel of food."[6] One Connecticut soldier had written, "Our clothes were very poor, the bare ground our couch, and the cold dews of heaven our only blanket."[7] The prisoners' only comforts were reading from their Testaments and occasionally singing together.

Months and months passed. Betsey waited, hoped, prayed. As the cold set in again, she worried that Abner had no comfortable shelter; but even Betsey, with all her concern, could not have imagined Abner's pitiful situation, his constant hunger, his weather-abused body, his pain, his sickness.

Another Christmas, 1864, another dreary season with no word from Abner. Was he still alive? Betsey was tormented to know the truth. Then the letter came. It was late in January, only a few days after their fifteenth wedding anniversary. A friend of Abner's at Andersonville Prison told Betsey what she had subconsciously feared but had refused to face. Abner had died of "chronic diarrhea" around September in the hospital at Andersonville. He was buried there in an unmarked grave.[8]

It was a fact: Abner was dead. Her poor young children were fatherless. Betsey's long-suppressed tears welled up from the depths. She mourned for her dear Abner. There was no marker yet in Georgia where Abner lay but, in Putnam, Connecticut, Betsey added a stone beside her children's. It was engraved simply "ABNER."

Detail of Betsey and Abner Lee's monument, with weather-worn engraving for Abner: "Died at Andersonville Prison Ga."

On February 3, 1865, Betsey, bundled in her coat and bonnet, with her black mourning dress underneath, set off for the neighboring town of Woodstock. She and her children were in dire need of money (she had not received any from her husband since his capture); now that her husband was dead, she was deserving of a pension. But Betsey was unaware of the massive amount of paperwork and documents to be completed and sent to the government to prove that she and her children were indeed the family of Abner Lee. That first day, Betsey answered the judge of probate's questions under oath the best she could, "that her said husband enlisted at Norwich on or about the 14th day of Dec A.D. 1863 for the term of 3 Years and continued in actual service in said war, for the term of about 10 mos and Died at Andersonville Ga on or about the ____ day of Sept A.D. 1864 and the cause of his death was Chronic diarrhea brought on by imprisonment, etc....That the names and age_ of her children

Andersonville Prison, August, 1864.
Collection of the National Archives, Records Administration (Item No. RG165-A-445), Washington, D.C.

Late-nineteenth-century view of Putnam, Connecticut.

under sixteen years of age at her husband's decease, and the place of her residence is as follows: Sarah I.J., 14, Phineas W, 11, Susie A.M. 9,, Leilia.N.L. 5, & Hattie I.L. 1 yrs old and all reside in Thompson, Ct." [9]

In good faith, Betsey spent days going through the necessary steps so she might receive her pension. But there was a problem. She knew her husband had died many months earlier, but the army did not. Abner Lee was still being reported "absent" on the monthly company muster roll. It was not until the end of the war, on the muster roll dated April 30, 1865, that Abner was finally reported to have "died at Andersonville Ga Oct-1/64 final statements sent." And it was not until May of 1865 that the Adjutant General's Office filed the Final Statement,[10] officially declaring Abner's death. At some time later, Betsey received her certificate for a pension of eight dollars per month. And on January 14, 1868, after filling out many more forms, Betsey was issued an additional two dollars monthly for each of her children under sixteen years of age.

That was not enough money, however, for her to provide for her family, and Betsey was soon forced to move to the center of the smoke-belching, busy industrial town of Putnam, near where her mother and brothers lived, and to take a job in the shoe manufactory there. Her life became one of long, grueling hours and drudgery as she struggled to earn enough to feed her children. Shortly, her eldest daughter Belle also began working there with her mother while fifteen-year-old Susanna kept house and took care of younger sisters Lillie and Hattie. During that difficult period, in April of 1872, Betsey's youngest child Hattie, only nine, died of scarlet fever. As if resigned and accepting the departure of those dearest to her, Betsey had the gravestone engraved

> Hatti shall not always sleep,
> Others for her must not weep
> In this world to come so bright
>   and fair
> We'll find our darling Hatti there.

🐝

> Remember the Sabbath day
> To keep it holy.

Betsey's mother had signed that on two different quilt blocks in 1846. In 1875, she too had died, and willed to her daughter her "Best Mirror, My piece of embroidery that her father's sister Worked, The Beaureau in the bedroom, one light stand, One Table-cloth that was my sisters my parlor carpet The Gold Beads that [were] her sisters, my two parlor tables." All her clothing, furniture, crockery and tinware were divided equally between Betsey and Betsey's eldest daughter, Belle. And, as was tradition, Betsey's brother Phineas, the elder son, inherited his mother's home.[11] But Phineas, as the good brother he was and a bachelor all his life, opened the house to Betsey, her youngest daughter Lillie having died, the other three children having grown and moved elsewhere.[12] Betsey and Phineas lived in their mother's large house, high on the hill overlooking the railroad tracks, the Catholic Church steeple of Putnam and the monstrous cotton mills. Betsey could look down to the shoe manufactory in the distance, and she could feel relief that she no longer had to work there.

For years Betsey had treasured her pile of signature blocks, each one signed carefully by her friends and family. But now they were yellowed with age, and some of the early fabrics were fragile.[13] She had long wanted to put them together into a quilt, but until now she had never had a moment to herself. As she laid out the blocks, many memories of happier times in her youth came to mind.

Miss Betsey M. Wright
Examin your Heart.
Theophilus B. Chandler.
Woodstock.
18th Sept. 1846

She came to the block her great-uncle had signed:

Miss Betsey M. Wright
Examin your Heart.
Theophilus B. Chandler.
Woodstock.
18th Sept. 1846

And Betsey remembered having seen oil portraits of his parents, her great-grandparents, Elizabeth Frink and Theophilus Chandler,[14] attired in their elegant English fineries: Elizabeth in a yellow silk brocade gown with a black lace shawl, small white cap and earrings; Theophilus in a powdered wig, blue single-breasted coat and crimson vest. Those portraits revealed to Betsey a glimpse of her proud heritage and the beginnings of the prominent Chandler family in America.

Their daughter Isabel Chandler May, Betsey's grandmother, had died when Betsey's mother, Sarah,

was only nine. It was for that reason that Sarah May had spent time in Fitzwilliam, New Hampshire, where her brother lived, and it was there that she had fallen in love with and married the doctor's fine son Phineas Wright, and later given birth to three children, Betsey, Phineas W. and Ebenezer. But, when Betsey was six, her grandfather, Doctor Ebenezer Wright, died, and her father immediately sold their property in Fitzwilliam, loaded all their possessions into the wagon and took Betsey, her brothers and mother south to Woodstock, Connecticut, where Betsey's mother's family, the Mays and Chandlers, all lived. There, her father bought the house in East Woodstock built by Betsey's great-great-grandfather John May in the early 1700's. For all these generations the May family had continued to live in this house on the gorgeous 185-acre

farm. The house was unique, and the family took great pride in it. The construction was superb and unusual for its period: spacious rooms, high ceilings with huge, hand-hewn beams, flooring of wide-planked pumpkin pine, a generous brick hearth in the kitchen with the beehive oven where the May women had cooked their meals for over one hundred years.

*I*n December of 1710, the same year this northern part of Woodstock was laid out, John May was already beginning this house. At that time he was one of only five men who could help one another against the ever-prevalent dangers of unfriendly Indians, wolves, wildcats and bears in this dense forest, but with their combined efforts they had cleared their land, planted and harvested their first crops, built their houses and prepared their flax for spinning.

When Betsey was young, she had practiced her letters over and over in any blank space she could find in the parchment pages of his diary. Later she may have tried to read some of John May's tiny script as he described building the house, from his going "a-logging" to finally "laying the hearth." It had taken him over one year to finish his clapboard home there on Muddy Brook.[15]

According to his diary, John May always kept the Sabbath Day. The Congregational Church was the focal point of his family's life, as it was in Betsey's. And Betsey remembered the invigorating one-half-mile ride from the May house to the First Congregational Church on those wintry Sabbath mornings, the sun glistening on the undisturbed, fresh-fallen snow, the air crisp, the scent of wood smoke emanating from passing chimneys. Only the muted clops of horses' hooves and the smooth, whistling glide of the sled runners had broken the silence. Many of those winter mornings, she had felt almost frozen to death by the time she had arrived at their destination. There was no heat in the church, and Betsey remembered the old straight-line pews once belonging to her grandfather Caleb May and the mist coming from everyone's face as each reverently shivered in silence.

How time had sped by since those carefree days of her childhood; how much sadness she had had to endure. Now Betsey was in her fifties. Many of the people who had signed her friendship blocks and most of her own family were gone. She must put her pieced blocks together into a finished quilt.

There were so many blocks. She spent hours planning where each one should go: her father, her mother, her sister, her Aunt Betsey. The blocks to go around the edge had to be cut in half, but Betsey carefully cut them straight across above the messages, so every word was left, secrets to her alone, since she would have to turn the messages under for the finished edge. Those verses would remain hidden forever in the hem of the quilt.[16]

She picked out a bright red, printed cotton for the sashing, a stylish, popular print in the 70's, and cut that into strips. Then Betsey began sewing her blocks together by hand with careful stitches.

For the quilt back, Betsey purchased yards of twenty-six-inch-wide cloth, tan with a small black dot. She proudly sewed the four widths together with her new Singer sewing machine, marveling at the speed with which she could finish a length of the backing. The same task would have taken many hours by hand in her youth. With the front and back finished, Betsey spread a cotton batt between them and quilted the whole very sparingly, only enough to keep it together, for this quilt was to be a sentimental keepsake, never a quilt for use. Finally, Betsey turned the top and back edges in to one another and stitched around the entire quilt with her Singer. It was difficult to finish the edges perfectly, especially the corners, and at times she did not catch both sides together. But it was only important to Betsey that her blocks were finally together after all these years, and now, instead of a box of delicate blocks in her chest, she had her heirloom quilt, her "album bed quilt"[17] that she should have put together before her wedding to Abner.

On December 30, 1887, Betsey made out her will. She listed each of her belongings separately, including "one album bed quilt" and a "Singer sewing machine."[18] At sixty-four years of age, she had amassed quite a collection of early treasures, along with her husband's belongings, and wanted each of her three surviving children and her grandchildren to have some heirloom of the May-Chandler-Wright families.

Several years later, from inside her house, Betsey gazed out over Putnam, the billowing smoke from the brick smokestacks of the cotton mills dispersing into the grim winter sky. Her children were all married and living in other towns; her son Phineas, in fact, had gone all the way to Oakland, California, with his wife and children. On the perch near her sat Betsey's companion, her brilliantly arrayed poll parrot. Betsey was tired. Her life had not always been as she had expected, nor as she had wanted, but she had been given the strength to endure.

Betsey was seventy-two. It was Christmas again, 1895, a half-century since her brother Phineas had given her that little friendship block inscribed "Betey! I wish you a merry christmas." But Betsey did not quite make Christmas that year; that Christmas, instead of a verse penned on cloth, a verse was forever chiseled in stone:

Sleep Mother sleep
   with your hands on your breast.
Poor weary Mother
   You needed your rest.
Well have we loved you,
   but God loved you best.
Tis thy God given rest.

A detail from Betsey's will, bequeathing her "album bed quilt."

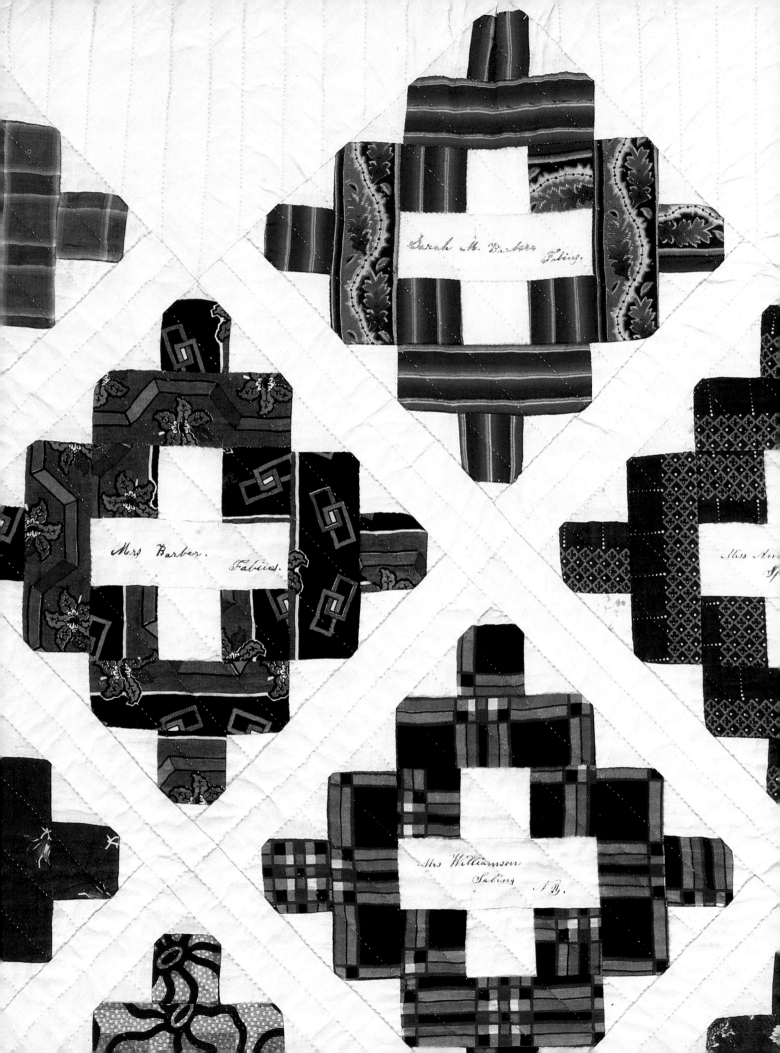

Scynthia Jane Risley
Fabius Onondaga Co.
N.Y.

ngsby
N.Y.

Aug Eve Stanley
Wisconsin

Miss Olive Barber
Fabius Onondaga Co.
N.Y.

Till Death Do Us Part

In a
peaceful little cove,
ensconced in wooded, roll-
ing hills, a simple New England-
style white Baptist church with stal-
wart steeple has loomed over the sleepy
community since 1819. The busy saw- and
gristmills, blacksmith shop, carding mills, tannery, wagon maker's, shoe shop, harness shop,
hattery, cooperage, distillery, fulling mill, cabinet
shop, general store, all those are gone; only
the church remains as it was. Now the land
is quiet, filled with pastoral scenes of generous, well-kept farms. And the sturdy, strug-
gling people of those bustling days are
silent too, their existence now marked
only by chiseled stones protruding
from the earth, the earth they
tediously, with strength and
energy, cleared.

Behind the church are many weather-worn tombstones, some small, others large, many in groupings of entire families lying side by side: infants, young sons and daughters, mother, father and grandparents. There is one prominent row by itself, midway back on the right-hand side of the church: early, unmatching, different-shaped stones, the first of a little eight-year-old boy of Alvin and Electa Blowers, next their infant son, then four larger stones: Dorothy, wife of Moses Blowers; Lucy, wife of Moses Blowers; Bathsheba, wife of Moses Blowers; a space, and Anna, wife of Moses Blowers. In the space between his first wife Bathsheba and the last, Anna, an entire stone lies on its back, the earth slowly consuming it. The stone is engraved, "Moses Blowers Died Nov. 9, 1863 Aged 88 yrs 11 mos." Except for these stones, the Blowers name is gone from that place now but has made a mark in the local history of Pompey, Delphi and Fabius, New York.

Moses Blowers (?).
Courtesy of Roy K. Blowers,
his great-great-grandson.

$\mathcal{M}$oses was a young, adventuresome lad of seventeen, the year 1792, when, with his axe and a pack of belongings and along with two other men, he left his home in White Creek, New York, near the Vermont border, and headed for this virgin frontier region. Upon arriving here, the three young men settled on lot 84 in Pompey Four Corners.[1]

Moses was well-secured, his log house built, and many acres cleared and planted five years later when he married eighteen-year-old Bathsheba Lewis, a newcomer from Shaftsbury, Vermont. At twenty-two, strong, enormous Moses promised his new bride a comfortable life, and the following year, on August 6, 1798, their first son Abel was born.

In the twenty-five years of their marriage, Bathsheba and Moses were blessed with eight healthy children, ranging from one and a half years to twenty-two, and a prosperous farm. The Baptist Church provided the structure in their lives, and Moses and Bathsheba and their children spent many hours there weekly. But in March of 1822, the neighborhood held an "awakening."

Early photograph of Main Street, Pompey, New York. Courtesy of Raymond W. Benson, Pompey Historical Society.

Bathsheba attended the emotional "hell-and-brimstone" revival and became inwardly troubled and depressed. From the *Onondaga Register* on April 10, 1822, several weeks after the awakening: "The Manlius paper of last week states, that the wife of Moses Blowers of Pompey, put an end to her natural life by drowning in a well, on the 28th ult. Mrs. Blowers was one of the subjects of an awakening which had been got up in the neighborhood, who fancied herself a sinner beyond the reach of mercy."[2]

Bathsheba's fourth child Alvin was fifteen at the time. He, and his brothers and sisters, painfully suffered feelings of loss and abandonment by their gentle, kind mother. Bewildered by his wife's suicide, Moses tried to give his children security and strength, but he was at a loss to fill the void she had left. He soon set out to find a woman to step into her place.

Fifteen months later, he married Bathsheba's first cousin Lucy Lewis. At twenty-five and only half her husband's age, Lucy took over the responsibilities of the household and of Bathsheba's children, also bearing three of her own. Sadly, though, six weeks after the birth of her third child in 1832, Lucy was laid to rest beside Bathsheba in the cemetery behind the church. Once again Moses was left with small children. This time, however, he did not need to remarry so quickly: with his children ranging from six weeks to thirty-two years, the older children could take care of the younger ones.

Almost three months after Lucy's death, Moses' and Bathsheba's son Alvin and daughter-in-law Electa had a darling little girl of their own. They named her Lucy Irena Blowers in memory of Moses' deceased second wife.

Alvin and Electa Blowers. Courtesy of Roy K. Blowers.

Chimney Sweep, *by Lucy Irena Blowers, Fabius, New York,*
c. 1849, 85 1/2 × 84 1/2 inches, pieced and appliquéd cottons.

$\mathcal{A}$t sixteen, Lucy Irena Blowers was a small, slim, sensitive girl with long jet-black hair and haunting gray eyes. Her entire world centered upon Fabius and Pompey, New York, with many friends and family there. Yet her father had finally made the decision to follow his brothers to Michigan,

and had announced to his family that they would be leaving as soon as he could settle his accounts, sell his land and get packed.

The thought of moving was traumatic to Lucy. She had lived in this magnificently hilly countryside all her life. Michigan was a long journey away, and she secretly feared

she might never see many of her New York family and dear friends again. Wanting to take something of her loved ones with her, Lucy began making a friendship quilt. She decided that this was to be a girls' quilt—for women only; she made only three exceptions: blocks for two small cousins in Cuba, New

York, and one special block for her little brother, Elbert.

Indeed, Elbert was very special to Lucy. Less than a year old and the baby of the family, he was all the more precious and fragile because his birth had softened some of the pain of her eight-year-old brother's death two years earlier. But Lucy also worried about little Elbert, for she was well aware how critical the first year of a child's life was. Her first baby brother had died when only six months old. Certainly Lucy loved little Elbert more than anything else in her life and, intending for him to have an important place on her quilt, Lucy wrote tenderly "My little Brother Elbert Duportal" onto a block pieced with a red, flowered calico.

Her grandfather, Moses Blowers, was celebrating his seventy-fifth birthday that very year. Only five years before, he had married another Lewis first cousin, Dorothy Stewart, his third wife. Lucy, who had never known her real grandmother, Bathsheba, nor her namesake Lucy Lewis, called Dorothy "Grandma," and Dorothy signed her block for Lucy's quilt "Grandma Blowers, Pompey, Onondaga Co., N.Y."

Lucy was proud of her Grandpa Blowers: he was such an unusual man. People had long ago given him the title of "Superman." At six feet eight, and 285 pounds, he had intimidated and towered over everyone in the community, including Lucy's own father, who had always felt small at only six feet three and 225 pounds. There were all kinds of stories about Moses Blowers: that he could bend ten-penny nails in his teeth, pick up a log with two men sitting on it or lift a barrel containing fifty-five gallons of pickles over his head and hold it in his teeth.[3] And, after more than half a century of work, Moses had made an impressive, large farm and

an enormous, three-story plank house with fireplaces upstairs and down. Surely, Lucy would miss her grandfather and this place. She had spent many happy hours of her childhood playing on the serene, grassy hillsides and forests with Moses' children, who were very close to her own age. In fact, Lucy's aunt Irena Blowers, who signed Lucy's quilt, was actually her playmate and only five years older than she.

*I*n 1849,[4] Lucy's quilt was finished. All sixty-one blocks had been pieced, signed and assembled into the top; Lucy carefully cut out green-sprigged cotton leaves in two different shapes and tediously appliquéd them around three sides. She basted the top to the thin cotton filling and minusculely dotted backing and then quilted the three layers together diagonally.

Lucy folded her masterpiece and carefully packed it in the wagon for the first leg of the long trip westward. At nearby Syracuse, her father transferred their belongings to the Erie Canal boat, its destination Lake Erie, where Lucy, her little brother Elbert in arms, Martin, Harriet and their mother and father boarded a steamboat for Detroit. The last leg of their trip was by stage to Hudson, Lenawee County, Michigan.

Those first years in Michigan were difficult for Lucy. Her parents, Alvin and Electa, single-handedly were running the Lenawee County Poor Farm: her father was in charge of the men and the farming, her mother of the women and girls, the cooking and cleaning. Without any previous training, her father

My Mother.

also had to act as the doctor, from amputating a gangrenous finger through a knothole in the woodshed wall with only his pocket knife to treating the sick and "insane."[5]

This was a sad time for Lucy, too. She had cuddled her little brother, rocked him, played with him, chased after him. But her little brother died that first year in Michigan, on November 22, 1850, not yet three years old. And he had lain in the tiny wooden coffin, silent, the rosy color whitewashed from his cheeks, his delicate fingers knotted into grotesque, lifeless fists. How could it be — her little brother, so healthy and strong, a constant joy in her life, had been taken away so permanently and so quickly?

In 1854, Lucy's father, Alvin, took his family to new government land he had bought several miles west of Hudson. Adjoining the land of his brother, it was on section

15, in Pittsford Township, Hillsdale County, Michigan. Alvin immediately erected a log house, later replaced by a nice frame one and a forty-foot barn and shed. The Michigan Southern and Northern Indiana Railroad Company rumbled through part of his land and, for $1.50 a cord, Lucy's father and uncle split beechwood and stacked it alongside the tracks for fuel.[5]

But Lucy was not living with her parents any longer. One year before, on December 29, 1852, she had married twenty-two-year-old William Henry Tolford, the boy who had lived three houses down the road from her in her old neighborhood. It had been a lovely, small wedding that Wednesday following Christmas at the Tolford house.[6] Henry and Lucy were so happy and in love, and made such a handsome couple as they had stood together before the Minister of the Gospel

repeating their vows. It was uncanny how they resembled one another, both of them with shiny black hair and gray eyes, Lucy petite and Henry somewhat taller at five feet eight.[7]

Lucy was proud to be Mrs. Tolford, and prouder still when the family doctor, Dr. Rice, delivered their dark-haired baby girl the following year, in May of 1854.

*T*he years passed and, in 1861, Lucy and Henry were well settled in their humble yet happy home with their three children: Mary, seven; Flora, four; and William A., two. But on June 20 of that year, Henry, along with Lucy's brother Martin, enlisted in the Fourth Michigan Regiment in the War of the Rebellion. Lucy dreaded to part with her husband; nevertheless, nearly three months later, in September, the two young patriots, Henry and Martin, enthusiastically and excitedly departed for their regiment in Detroit. They were off to see the sights: Washington, D.C. and the warm South, places they had never hoped to see in a lifetime. And, besides that, they were men fighting for a cause they believed in. Hour by hour, the days passed ever so slowly without her Henry, and Lucy lived from day to day with the hope of another letter from her husband or brother.

But, as the days slowly became months, so did Lucy's slim figure gradually change, and she fondly remembered those last nights before her Henry had departed. Seven months after he had left, in March of 1862, Henry sent a message to Lucy that he was very sick and in the camp hospital. And in May, Henry was sent home on sick leave until he was fully recovered and able to return to duty.

It seemed an answer to Lucy's prayers to have her husband home now that she was eight months pregnant. Tiring quickly, Lucy found it more and more difficult to take care of the children, keep house, tend to the garden and keep them all fed and in dresses and pantaloons. Of course, Henry could not be of much help to her physically; he was so weakened from disease. She would, in fact, have one more person to care for. But Henry was there, at least, and for his warm support and company she was overjoyed.

As the weeks passed, Henry regained his strength. By mid-June, Henry was troubled that in all good faith he should write to his commanding officer about his restored health and should return soon to the regiment; yet, he could not leave his wife in her condition. She was huge with child, and due to go into labor at any moment. He was in a dilemma. Finally, on June 25, 1862, Henry did what he felt was honest: he wrote to the colonel of his regiment, hoping for a sympathetic reaction to his circumstances.

Hudson June 25th 1862
Col. J.R. [?]. Dear Sir,
   Private
Henry Tolford of Co. F. 4th Mich Infantry (home on sick leave) would respectfully report himself as able for duty, and ask for transportation papers to enable him to return to his regiment. If any writing is needed to present to the Pay-Master in order to draw my regular pay, please furnish me with the same as my family are very much in want of it. I should like very much to remain at home ten days longer on account of my wifes health if proper to do so. Please let me know what you think of it.
   Respectfully yours
   Wᵐ H.. Tolford
P.S. Please direct to Hudson Lenawee Co Mich[8]

Only three days after Henry wrote this letter, Lucy gave birth to a baby girl, Caroline Estelle. A few days later, the dreaded letter from the regiment arrived. Lucy fearfully waited to hear Henry's orders: thankfully, Henry was not to return to the regiment until September.[8]

September had seemed so distant to Lucy then. Without her Henry, the months had seemed an eternity; yet the months with Henry hurriedly melted away. All too soon, now, August was passing; little Estelle was two months old already. Lucy tried to savor every moment with her husband those last days. She could not bear to part with him again. But Henry was a soldier first, with the cause of freedom—emancipation—stirring him onward; he must go.

Several weeks later, Lucy and her parents received a letter from Lucy's brother Martin, dated August 25, 1862. Now Martin was very sick in the camp hospital. Henry had visited him on the way back to the regiment, so Martin mentioned in the letter that Henry had just left.[5]

Although overwhelmed with work, with a baby and three older children, Lucy was constantly lonely. After having Henry there with her, she found it difficult again to adjust to stark paper and ink. Lucy thought of Henry, so far away in Virginia, and she wished he could see little Estelle's first tottering steps, or hear their four-year-old son's "grown-up" conversations, or see pretty Flora and Mary in their best calico dresses for church. Henry was missing all this. The years were passing, Lucy's family separated, her children growing up without their father.

In January of 1864, Henry's enlistment term was nearly over; he would soon be coming home. Lucy

was so thankful and relieved that her Henry was one of the men to be returning, and she counted the days until he would finally be home for good.

To her utter disappointment, however, Henry wrote that he had re-enlisted. Of course it was with the stipulation that he would for certain "have a furlough of at least thirty days in his state." [9] He would be home on leave at the end of February for thirty-five days.

*T*heir visit seemed so brief. Henry was a complete stranger to his toddler, Estelle ; Flora, Mary and William had grown and changed

Martin Blowers, c. 1861–1865.
Courtesy of Roy K. Blowers.

so since he had last seen them. Lucy, beautiful and slim as ever, looked older now too, fine lines of worry on her forehead, and deep concern in her teary gray eyes.

Henry took Lucy in his arms and kissed her good-bye, promising the war would soon be over, and he would return to her. Then he left on the train, once again for the regiment, and on his way he planned to spend a day or so in Baltimore cheering Lucy's brother Martin who, still convalescing, was now a hospital orderly.

His spirits lifted after Henry's visit, Martin wrote an unusual letter all in rhyme to his parents and Lucy :

The visit was with Henry made
To see him I was very glad
Both for his sake and that he'd come
Directly from loved ones at Home ;
And as you say, he much could tell
"Of things you could not write so well."
He arrived on Friday safe and sound
And me without much trouble found.
That afternoon we both went out
And in the City looked about.
Among the places to which we went
Was the Washington Monument
Where climbing up the lofty height
A prospect fine did greet our sight.
In the evening went out together
Notwithstanding stormy weather
To Maryland Institute Hall
Where we heard there had been a call
For a great meeting to be held
The purpose of which was to weld
The Union men so fast and firm
That they will make the Rebels squirm
And beat them bad on Wednesday next
With Emancipation as the text.
For on that day is an Election
For the calling a Convention
Which shall, at the earliest date,
Abolish Slavery through the State
The speakers were fearless and bold
And the truth right plainly told.
Winter Davis of Maryland
Was the first upon the stand
He spoke in his own cogent style
And had attention from all, the while.

Boutwell next, from the Yankee nation
Dug deep about Truth's foundation.
And then a man from Keystone State
Some funny stories did relate.
His name, I think was Amos Myer.
Though long his speech it did not tire.
Then came Lew Wallace — type of the West,
And the meeting briefly addressed
In words of eloquence and power
Upon the question of the hour.
But I will not attempt to write
Of all we saw and heard that night,
But let it now suffice to say,
That well pleased we came away,
That you may see how stern War teaches
I'll send a paper with these speeches.
I believe the time is near at hand
When Freedom'll reign in Maryland!
Success we say to Emancipation
And that too "without compensation."
So work goes on for God hath spoken
Let every Tyrants yoke be broken.
It is the War that rends it Twain
Slavery's vile and monstrous chain!
Who'll now oppose that grand decree
"Loose the bonds, let the oppressed go free"?
Saturday P.M. Henry went on
The 3 o'clock train to Washington
For his visit I thankful feel
And think he too enjoyed it well.
May God his life still kindly spare
And ever have him in his care
And the happy time soon come
When he'll return to friends and Home. [10]

Several weeks later, Martin wrote that Henry had been promoted to corporal.

Lucy had not heard from her husband for several weeks and was growing concerned when (about six weeks after Lucy had last seen him) she received a letter in mid-May 1864 from H. Lewis, a friend of Henry's.

Lucy stared in disbelief, her vision blurring: May 5, 1864... Henry...fracture of the leg... killed in battle...field near Spotsylvania Court House...at Wilderness Farm, Va.[11]

She read the letter over and over again, the meaning not penetrating, weakness and numbness overtaking her body. Henry gone? The tears came, tears that would never stop— outwardly yes, but inwardly never.

Her parents tried to comfort her, providing a warm home for Lucy and the four children. But Lucy, draped in black crepe, her eyes red and swollen, mourned and could not be consoled. She had waited, she had hoped, she had prayed, but now she had no more hope: she would never see Henry again—at least, not in this world.

Lucy's mother could not bear to see her daughter and grandchildren in such pain, and expressed herself in two letters to her son Martin, who was still working in a Baltimore hospital after his illness, unable to return to the front.

Hudson   May 29 1864

My Dear Son,

After the lapse of another week, I again have recourse to my pen to commit a few thoughts to paper for your perusal, and to acknowledge the receipt of your kind letter which came to hand on Friday Eve, contents eagerly perused, thank you for the love and sympathy expressed and also for the Interest manifested in Home duties. I feel that we do indeed need your assistance in many things and more particularly since our recent affliction. My health has improved

I feel much better than I did two months ago. Pa keeps trying to work every day, but says he feels bad most of the time that he does not feel able to work, I think he is discouraged, I think if you were Home to help him, it would do him more good than Medicine. He with the rest of us feels that we have been called to mourn the loss of one who was dear to us all, and an irreparable loss to his Dear family. He was an affectionate Husband, a kind tender Father, and when I look upon those little ones, (made Orphans by this wicked rebellion) and think how much they will need a Fathers care and protection through life, it brings tears to my eyes. Not only his family and friends have sustained a great loss But the Church of Christ, of which he was a worthy member....I wish the Lieut.[12] could find out more particulars by this H. Lewis. I suppose if the wound was a fracture of the leg, that he died from loss of blood, feel as though it would be a great satisfaction to know just how

long he lived, if he appeared to suffer a great deal, What he said in his dying moments, and particularly if he left any message for his family & friends and to ascertain if he was really buried and his grave marked. Some would think those things of small account.

I should think it would be best for you to write to Washington to find out about his Bounty—he has not had any of his or US reenlistment Bounty nor State or Local Bounty, I suppose she Lucy will draw a pension from Government I dont know how much she is entitled to. He had not drawn any pay since they went back, think they were paid up to the 1st of April. Lucy has had one payment of eight dollars, from Detroit, from the fund for Soldiers Families and Henry got the same before he went from Detroit, put enough with it to make thirty and sent back, he said they agreed to give her eight dollars per month, but we would have to write every month in order to get it. it is about time to write again. dont

know whether she will get this now or not. Mrs Tolford thought she would draw pay one year after his death. . . .[13]

Hudson July 26th/64

My Dear Son,

. . . I attended Church Sabbath day Eld. Pack preached an excellent Sermon in the A.M. Eld. Woodworth preached at three o'clock P.M. He is a smart man but is as comical as ever. he talked some about the War, and the new call. He told some plain truths, that were not calculated to help the secession sympathizer. I think from what I have heard, that this late call for more men, is troubling a good many about here, some few that are able are Buying Substitutes at a great price will be a hard matter to find men that will go as substitutes for drafted Men There are some left about here yet, that perhaps would not have to sacrifice any more than some that have gone. Dr. Rice was here to day said the Draft would have to come <u>off</u> this time with out doubt. There has been two or three War Meetings in Hudson, there is going to be a Meeting at the Town house to morrow P.M. The Draft dont excuse Veterans but one year, I have been told. Mr Woodworth said he thanked God, that there were <u>some</u> that thought more of the <u>principles</u> of our Republican Institutions, than they did of their own lives. I hope and pray that this year may end the War.

The Blood and Tears that have been shed, the Misery & Anguish that this War has caused, no <u>human</u> heart can conceive. . . .

There are a great many that call themselves loyal, now begin to think they are in danger, you can see their <u>bump</u> of Selfishness developed amazingly, sometimes I am almost inclined to laugh, and then a feeling of contempt to see the shifts and turns that people would be glad to make to get rid of going. I feel same as Mr Woodworth expressed himself Sunday. He was speaking of the <u>long faces</u> since the last call, says, "Do you suppose the wives and Mothers are weeping, because there is another call for more Men, while their Husbands, and Sons are standing before the Cannon's mouth and needing help, said, "They had a right to weep for Joy, I believe there are a great many, that would rather give up our Liberty and free Institutions and submit to tyranny, then to put themselves in the way of danger.

I do not feel so, I think we have sacrificed too much already as a

family, to give up now. There has been too much precious blood spilled to give up now. They did not make out much to the meeting this P.M. There is a great excitement about it. The topic of conversation is about the Draft. . . .

Thurs. Eve. Lucy & Amelia have been up to George's to day. they said that John & Carrie were in Elmira, NY went there to escort some Rebel prisoners. . . .

Mr Harmon Webb was here this morning he said that the <u>News</u> came to Hudson yesterday that the Rebels was making another raid into Maryland toward Washington and had taken one or two whole Brigades of our men.[14]

Lucy and her mother and father were later to hear only the most terrifying reports of Henry's death and of the Battle of the Wilderness — that Grant's army, numbering over 100,000 men, had made contact with the Confederate forces on Henry's fateful day, May 5, 1864, in "dense thickets where orderly battle plans were impossible."[15] "A nightmare of bloodshed made more terrible by the fact that the woods caught fire and many of the wounded were suffocated or burned to death."[16] On the first two days of fighting (May 5 and 6), 2,246 Union soldiers were killed; one of those was Lucy's beloved Henry.

Indeed, with that dreaded news, Lucy would never know what had been Henry's final doom. She prayed he had not suffered in the end, that he had been buried decently. But thoughts of the horrors of that battle continually tortured her.

And time did not heal Lucy's grief. One year — two years — three. Her older children were growing up into adolescents, teenagers, the baby going to school; yet Lucy continued to grieve. Still she suffered the fresh, strong pangs of the loss of her husband.

Six years after her husband's death, at thirty-eight Lucy was still beautiful and slim — maybe too slim, her defenses too weakened from her great sadness — when typhoid fever spread through this rural community. At first, Lucy was unaware she was sick. She had aches and pains and trouble sleeping at night, then a slight fever and overall tiredness. But, by the end of that first week, her fever high and climbing, Lucy was forced to go to bed while her parents cared for her and the four children. Lucy only grew worse. Dr. Rice, the family doctor who had delivered each of Lucy's four babies, was called in, but his treatment was ineffective too. By the third week, Lucy was emaciated and exhausted. Dr. Rice and Lucy's parents hoped and prayed for a change for the better: Dr. Rice had known other patients to begin to recover slowly during the third or fourth week, and he was optimistic that Lucy also would. But, hourly, they stood by helpless as Lucy drew closer and closer to her death.

Alvin and Electa felt they could not bear to watch their daughter's hideous suffering any longer. Finally, on October 12, 1870, Lucy's frail body froze in long-sought peace.

Lucy died of typhoid fever that day, leaving her four weeping children in the care of her mother and father. Dr. Rice was there when Lucy died and "noted her death in [his] notebook at the time."[17] Lucy's death was also noted in the township records. But, as the years passed, Lucy's typhoid was forgotten. It was remembered only that Lucy had died so young, that she died presumably because she had lost the will to live without her dear Henry.

Steeple of Baptist church, Delphi Falls, New York.

Charcoal-enhanced photograph of Betsey J. Bills at the time of her marriage.

Save
the
Pieces

1849

With her nib-tipped pen and indelible ink, nineteen-year-
old Betsey Jane Bills ever so carefully copied the information
basted to each quilt block onto the blank white center square of
that block. This was not an easy task, and Betsey took her job very
seriously. She felt pride in the fact that her aunts here in Milford had
chosen her to inscribe their friendship blocks. Of course, she knew it was
because she was the schoolteacher in nearby Amherst, and as a teacher
she was expected to have beautiful handwriting. Certainly, she did not
want to embarrass herself by ruining a quilt block with a misspelled
name or blob of ink. As Betsey wrote, she was entertained by
her aunts' gossip and news of the family. Living a few

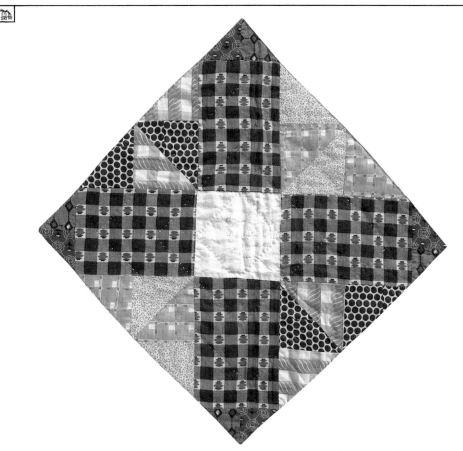

miles away in Amherst with her parents, Betsey missed out on a lot of the news of Milford, and she enjoyed hearing what each of her relatives was doing: "Rebecca Crosby is getting married." "The Cutlers had another baby: named him David." "Aunt Mary Minot is expecting again."[1]

Except for Betsey's own family, nearly all of her mother's side of the family lived in Milford, and several of them even lived side by side. Betsey's Uncle Joseph and Aunt Isabel Moore Crosby were next-door neighbors to her aunts Betsey Fifield and Dorothy Lund, and Aunt Harriet and Uncle Freeman Crosby lived nearby in the old family homestead on the land known for generations as the Crosby Farm. In fact, only one of Betsey's mother's ten brothers and sisters had moved away: Rachel Orinda Crosby had gone west to Indiana to teach school as soon as she had finished Ipswich Ladies' Seminary, and later she married a Reverend Sneed. And

it was Rachel's daughter's block that Betsey now sat at the table inscribing. From the basted note she copied "Anna C. Sneed, Godfrey, Illinois."

Betsey always enjoyed visiting her aunts, uncles and cousins in Milford. The Crosbys were such a close-knit, gregarious family. And it was fun to be involved in Aunt Isabel's friendship quilt project. Betsey loved and respected Aunt Isabel:[2] she was so optimistic, so positive, and always doing something nice for others, just as she was doing now, organizing this friendship quilt for her Crosby sisters-in-law. She had certainly suffered more than her share of troubles, with three of her four children dying so young. Her three-year-old, Helen Frances, had died only two years earlier, yet Isabel remained a pillar of the family and of the First Congregational Church of Milford.

Betsey noticed that Isabel's quilt block with twenty-nine pieces was

very different from all the others there on the table: they followed the friendship block pattern currently popular in New England. Instead of using two co-ordinating printed cottons, as everyone else had, Aunt Isabel had used seven different prints probably precious and meaningful only to her. Betsey did not inscribe that block; Aunt Isabel had already written a practical saying with underlying strength: "Save the pieces. I.M. Crosby Milford N H."

There were five blocks for her Aunt Betsey Fifield's family, however, that Betsey needed to inscribe. After redipping her nib into the ink, Betsey penned one block with Aunt Betsey's name, one for her fifteen-year-old son Charles and one for one-year-old Eliza Jennie. Then, sadly, there were two more: a memorial block for Warren F., Aunt Betsey's three-year-old who had died nine years earlier, and one for Harriet M., her two-year-old daughter gone now three years. Under each name, Betsey penned "Lowell, Mass.," where her aunt's family had lived until their recent move to Milford. Since these two children were buried in Lowell, perhaps the blocks on the quilt would serve in some small way as an outward expression of their mother's love for them.

After hours of writing, Betsey finally finished inscribing the blocks. Her aunts laid those, as well as a few blocks signed and sent to the Crosbys beforehand, in alternating rows of five and six, and then pieced the top. Next, there was a Crosby family quilting: a social gathering that had been taking place on that very land for nearly one hundred years, all the way back to Betsey's first Crosby ancestors to come to Milford, her great-great-grandparents Sarah Fitch and Josiah Crosby.

Album Patch, by the Crosby family women,
Milford, New Hampshire, c. 1849,
99 × 94 inches, pieced cottons,
cut for a poster bed.

𝒜 colorful picture had always been painted of Betsey's great-great-grandfather Josiah. His father had been killed by Indians, and young Josiah had been apprenticed to wheelwright Joseph Fitch of Bedford. Then, at eighteen years of age, seeming to be determined to avenge the death of his father, in 1748 he went out onto the frontier near the Connecticut River as a soldier.[3]

Nearly a century later, in 1831, the Concord newspaper had written: "He, with fifteen more, . . . fell into an ambush of one hundred and twenty Indians and French, who rose and fired. The commanding officer ordered each man to take care of himself. . . . Crosby ran up the river towards Fort Dummer, followed by an Indian, who coming up within a few rods of him, discharged his piece at him. The ball passed near his right ear; he then turned and fired at the Indian, who fell, and he saw no more of him. He pursued his way up the river until he came opposite Fort Dummer, where he attempted to swim the river, but before he could reach the opposite shore his strength failed him, and he sank to the bottom and was taken out by some men from the fort."[4]

Josiah later returned to the Fitches', completed his apprenticeship and married Mr. Fitch's daughter Sarah. From his new father-in-law, he purchased seventy-seven acres of unknown, unbroken forest bordering the Souhegan River in Amherst (now Milford), New Hampshire.[5]

In 1753, "on the back of one horse he packed his worldly possessions, his young wife and a son of 10 months, and mounted the steed, bade farewell to family and home and started off to the wilderness.

"There were no roads to follow in the latter part of the journey and this family trio found their way by blazed trees with musket in hand; an eye out for any unfriendly traveler, this brave pioneer pushed on, cheered by his young wife, who

divided her attention between her husband and babe.

"The Souhegan river was the goal of their ambitions, and when reaching the lively stream they unpacked, built a loghouse and set up a home in the forest,"[6] the beginnings of the Crosby Farm.

They traveled by "spotted trees" and lived on "salt pork, corn meal and bean porridge till the trees gave place to the log house, a patch of potatoes, and young cattle."[7] In their log house there was "room for a kitchen and bed-room, below which was a cellar reached through a trap-door, and a garret with a movable ladder as an elevator. The kitchen was always the sleeping-room" and the bedroom a gathering place, except when company came. "The early barns were rude structures, but were succeeded by framed buildings earlier than the log house, which was after extended to double size before the framed

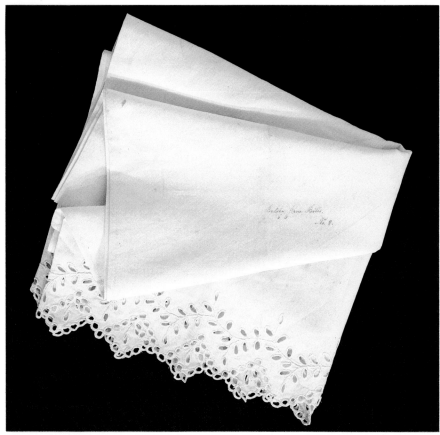

Betsey's eyelet-embroidered pillowcase, with her ink signature and number.

house appeared. . . . Their shelled corn bins [were] made of sections of hollow logs, fitted with bottoms and of the height of barrels."[8] There were no roads, schools or churches. Josiah and Sarah made their own clothing, raised their own food, made their own roads and taught their own children to read and write.

Of Sarah and Josiah's ten children, four went off with their in his parents' log house, "married at twenty-two years of age, and settled upon a lot of land upon a hill not far from his father's."[10]

Josiah II's wife, Elizabeth Littlehale, "received very small outfit as a marriage portion — a feather bed, a spinning-wheel, and perhaps a half-dozen sheep, as many chairs, a table and dishes to spread it, a chest with homespun clothes and a wedding-go-to-meeting suit."[11]

care for, and all the cooking and washing to do; a cow to milk; the poultry and pigs to feed; the wool and flax to spin, and cloth to weave; the stockings, buskins and mittens to knit, and sewing to do." Elizabeth kept "her dyepot in her chimney corner, and knew how to cheat the poor clothier, as he was called, out of the profit of coloring the stockings and mits of the household."[13]

Early view across the Souhegan River to the land known as the Crosby Farm,
where most of Betsey's maternal aunts and uncles lived. Courtesy of Barbara Crosby Enright.

father to the Revolutionary War. On June 17, 1775, Captain Josiah and two of his sons fought at the Battle of Bunker Hill, and it was there that Josiah sustained losses of "1 pistol and 1 pair of worsted stockings."[9] Josiah was later chosen to be a representative to the General Court of New Hampshire for the years 1778 and 1779.

Betsey's great-grandfather Josiah (II) was that ten-month-old baby who was with his father and mother on their first journey to Amherst by horseback in 1753. He grew up

Elizabeth's husband, Josiah II, was a farmer "long before a plow could be used, and ox-carts were scarce. Men carried their corn to the mill at great distances on their shoulders. . . . All labor was performed under great discouragements and disadvantages, so that full twenty years of hard toil and exposure gave only sufficient time to bring the farms into comfortable and remunerative condition."[12]

And Elizabeth's work was also difficult and endless. "She had her husband to cheer; her children to

Josiah II and Elizabeth had eleven children. "In due time he opened his house to his second son, Joseph," Betsey's grandfather. The old rule was for "one child to remain at home so that the fire should not go out under the old people, the well become dry or there 'be no herd in the stall.' "[14]

So, in this house of Josiah II's, Betsey's grandfather Joseph Crosby and grandmother Anna Conant lived and raised another eleven children, including Betsey's mother. And most of these eleven children were being represented on the family friendship quilt that the Crosbys were busy creating in 1849. In fact, Betsey's mother's sister Harriet Crosby lived in the house that had been built around part of Josiah II's original frame house. She had married her cousin Freeman Crosby, whose father had been the son to inherit the homestead; and

With renewed inspiration, Betsey returned to her parents' clapboard house on the ridge above beautiful colonial Amherst. Her father and brothers were farmers, and their plowed and planted acres of land in the midst of still primitive forested hillsides were proof of their continuous toil.

For nine more years, Betsey

Betsey's pantaloons.

Freeman and Harriet Crosby had always shared their grandfather's long, added-on house with Freeman's twin brother's family, whose names were also included on the blocks of the friendship quilt. Indeed, this homestead, and her Crosby ancestors, were Betsey's roots, and she was very proud of that legacy.

lived there with her mother and father, her three brothers and sister, Lucy, having married and moved into their own homes. And for nine school years, petite Betsey worked to impart her knowledge of reading, writing and arithmetic to her scholars in the cramped, one-room schoolhouse in the village of Amherst.

JUNE 14, 1859

Betsey carefully stepped into her white cotton pantaloons. She had made them herself, each stitch minuscule and perfectly straight. The scalloped, eyelet-embroidered edge looked so pretty over her knitted stockings. She pulled the ties at each side of her waist tight and made them into bows. She was slim now, but her mother's pattern certainly gave her room to expand, with the long ties and open sides. Over her head Betsey slipped on her best dress. It rustled elegantly as she straightened it and hooked the handsome collar which had been tediously cut and worked. Betsey was nearly ready. Her long, brown-black hair was parted in the middle, pulled back and tightly secured in a bun. One last thing: she must not forget her best earrings, for this was Betsey's long-awaited wedding day.

At twenty-eight, Betsey felt she had taught school long enough, nearly ten years now. Many of her own scholars were grown, even betrothed or married. But she had not waited in vain for a husband, for thirty-five-year-old Charles was a fine man and a successful farmer.

Betsey hurried downstairs where the minister and gathering of family and friends were waiting. Quickly and nervously, she responded to the vows and was Mrs. Charles W. Patterson.

Shortly after their joyous wedding celebration, Charles took his new bride several miles east to his farm on the road to the ferry landing in Thornton's Ferry (Merrimack), New Hampshire.

Betsey stood at the side of her husband's frame New England–style farmhouse and looked out over the valley. Several hundred feet in front of her were the tracks of the Boston and Maine Railroad headed for Concord or Nashua. Just below that, on the other side of the woods, was her new neighbor, the mighty Merrimack River.

Upon entering the house, thoroughly domesticated Betsey went to housekeeping, cleaning and then arranging her belongings, rearranging the kitchen in the back with her own crockery, pots, utensils and silverware, and making up the feather bed in the downstairs bedroom with her handmade linen sheets, bedding and eyelet-embroidered pillowcases she had made many years earlier for her hope chest. The rooms were small compared to the fine eighteenth-century colonial homes in Amherst, yet Betsey was comfortable — as comfortable as she could be on those sticky-hot summer days.

But fall soon came. With frosted windowpanes on those crisp mornings, the warmth of the potbellied stove in the kitchen felt good. Bet-sey was contented and cozy inside her neat, tidy little house, with the delicious aroma of bread baking or meat boiling as she sat knitting woolen socks and mitts for Charles.

Betsey wanted children. With the large families of the Bills and Crosbys, she had not considered she might have difficulty getting pregnant. But by June of 1861, Betsey and Charles were already married two years, and they still lived alone. Their house was beginning to feel so empty, and too quiet. But then the silence was interrupted by the foreboding, tremulous rumbling of the train loaded with young, enthusiastic soldiers headed for war, and Betsey's pangs of fear became terror that seized her insides and sickened her.

She and Charles talked about the war. "No," he reassured Betsey, he would not have to go. The war would not last that long. There were more than enough volunteers. Young men were excited, even anxious to join the army and see the country. Besides, he was thirty-seven years old.[15]

Still the train kept passing. More soldiers, mostly young men and boys, but now those boys were disheartened, scared — Shiloh, Bull Run, Antietam — one bloody battle after another, with thousands of men dying in each. Would there be no end?

In the fall of 1862, however, Betsey's pantaloons were getting tighter and tighter. She was no longer so slim. In fact, Betsey knew that there would come a time soon when her pantaloons would no longer fit at all. And she was delighted: she was going to have a baby.

On March 2, 1863, a crimson, wrinkled baby boy broke the silence with a shattering cry in the Patterson home. He was named John

Betsey wearing her apron, with a visitor, in front of her home in Thornton's Ferry, New Hampshire.

Henry. But the headlines of the newspapers several days later rekindled Betsey's terror. On March 3, the day after the birth of her son, Congress passed the national draft law, and President Lincoln made clear that that law would be enforced.

In the distance Betsey heard the familiar whistle, a call of doom and foreboding. Would her own husband be one of those soldiers passing by on that train soon?

And Betsey was thankful for her healthy son. She had even begun to accept the thought that little John would be an only child, when she discovered she was pregnant again. So, two years after the war's end, in August of 1867, Betsey was again giving birth. Once again a baby boy was placed into Betsey's arms, little Charles Frederick. As with her first child, Betsey prayed for her infant's life. So many mothers lost their babies: poor Aunt Isabel

becoming doctors, going "about doing good."[16]

Betsey threaded her needle with black embroidery floss and stitched a date into each empty space under "Deaths" on her sampler. She had begun this "Family Record" many years ago; at that time there were only a few dates under "Deaths," but slowly, certainly, over the years that column too had been filled in. Finally, and sadly, after so many years, with her Aunt Mary's death, she had finished her sampler; yet there was still one blank place remaining—the space after her own name, "Betsey Jane Bills." She would certainly never be able to fill that one in.

Family Record.

Births.		Deaths.		Births.		Deaths.
Ebenezer Bills	Mar 25 1760	Mar 13 1822.		Joseph Crosby	Oct 9 1774	May 23 1838.
Hannah Bullard	Aug 20 1767	Mar 6 1849.		Anna Conant	Oct 30 1780	Oct 20 1843.
Mianda Bills	Nov 5 1785	May 10 1834.		Nancy Crosby	Sept 27 1801	Dec 20 1874.
Rebecca Bills	Oct 3 1787	Sept 1 1857.		Harriet Crosby	Oct 20 1802	Sept 7 1855.
Lucy Bills	Nov 6 1789	Apr 26 1864.		Lucy Crosby	Aug 29 1804	Sept 28 1882.
Shubael Bills	Jan 3 1791	May 31 1850.		Joseph Crosby	Mar 3 1806	May 23 1892.
Jabez Bills	Dec 6 1793	Nov 12 1857.		Benj. Crosby	Oct 7 1807	Sept 23 1891.
Philinda Bills	Apr 15 1795	Mar 14 1845.		Josiah Crosby	Nov 12 1809	May 10 1863.
Sophronia Bills	Mar 31 1798	Apr 10 1886.		Betsey Crosby	Feb 26 1812	Nov 16 1888.
Samantha Bills	Mar 31 1798	May 21 1889.		Rachel Crosby	Aug 12 1813	Oct 21 1892.
Jesse Bills	Aug 15 1802	Dec 25 1851.		Abel C. Crosby	Nov 28 1815	July 12 1901.
Mark Bills	Apr 8 1806	Aug 26 1853.		Mary Crosby	Oct 12 1817	Feb 23 1907.
Hamilton Bills	July 8 1808	Feb 11 1841.		Deborah Crosby	Dec 8 1819	Sept 7 1866.

Jabez Bills
Lucy Crosby
Married Oct 29 1822

Births.		Deaths.
Aug 30 1823	Frederick J. Bills	Dec 4 1899.
Oct 6 1825	Freeman C. Bills	Apr 19 1894.
Feb 5 1829	Lucy A. M. Bills	July 12 1896.
Dec 16 1830	Betsey Jane Bills	
Nov 15 1834	George M. Bills	June 10 1863.

Married:
F.C.Bills & C.J.Twiss
B.B.Putnam & L.A.M.Bills
J.F.Bills & L.J.Wheeler
G.M.Bills & M.Baldwin
C.W.Patterson & Betsey J.Bills

Birth.		Death.
Harriet A. Bills	Apr 13 1835	Oct 22 1856.

Holy Bible

But sometimes Betsey could forget the frightful times. Little John greeted her each morning with bright eyes and a gleeful smile, naïve and innocent of the outside world. Healthy and strong, he seemed to change daily. He was crawling, then pulling himself up on chairs and tables, and finally walking. John was soon two years old, and the war was finally coming to an end. There had even been talk of an armistice. Finally Betsey could breathe more easily. Her prayers had been answered: it looked as if Charles would not be going to war after all.

had given birth to five, but only her daughter Esther was still alive; even Isabel's adopted, sixth child had died at seven months of age. How could Betsey be so fortunate? *Both* of her children were healthy.

1907

Looking back on the intervening years, Betsey remembered the joys of motherhood with two active, happy little boys. Her husband and she had been so proud of them. And their boys had grown up into fine men, both of them

JANUARY 1914

Silver-haired Betsey was eighty-four. As she studied the heirloom Family Record she had made, Betsey was filled with sadness. She had outlived them all—her brothers and sisters, aunts and uncles, mother and father, her husband, her fine sons, doctors Charles and John, both of whom had died so young. Yes, they had all gone on ahead. Then her eyes focused on the rebus she had carefully embroidered years earlier: "And when the [cross] we cease to bear A [crown] of life we hope to wear." Suddenly an inner smile and peace filled her; Betsey knew she would soon join her loved ones once again—this time forever.

Several years before her death, Betsey had begun her will, "Realizing the uncertainty of life and wishing to settle my worldly estate while I have the strength and capacity so to do and being of sound mind and memory, do make publish and declare this my last will and testament...."

After giving directions as to how her stone was to be cut, and after bequeathing money to the First Congregational Church of Merrimack and the public library there, Betsey willed to family members "the Carpet that was once her [Mary K. Putnam's] mothers and the featherbed in my bedroom, my Marble Top Black Walnut furniture Set, with Bed and Bedding as it stands, all the White Crockery with a green sprig, two large hooked rugs in parlor and the best ones in the sitting room, all my stockings, woolen or cotton home knit or boughten, with yarns, the bureau in the bed room, which is more than a hundred years old, the Gilt Framed Mirror, four Sterling Silver Forks, spoons," as well as the "rest of my silverware and old Desk."

Then Betsey finished: "Not wishing or desiring that any of my wearing apparel, or bedding, or table linen, or table furnishing,

Betsey, later in life.
Courtesy of Ida Putnam Stow, a grandniece.

should be sold at public auction, I hereby devise and desire that Annie M. Stark, Mary K. Putnam, and Jane E. Putnam [her nieces], meet, select and divide such articles as they desire, . . . the residue and remainder they do not wish, they may give to any one who they think would be pleased to receive them and use them with care for my sake."[17] Betsey's sampler, pantaloons and a pillowcase were included in this.

Now, in remembrance of Betsey, the missing piece can be added to her sampler: Betsey Jane Bills <u>Mar</u> <u>10</u> <u>1914</u>. She is buried in Last Rest Cemetery in Merrimack, New Hampshire, directly across from the First Congregational Church of which she was a member for so many years.

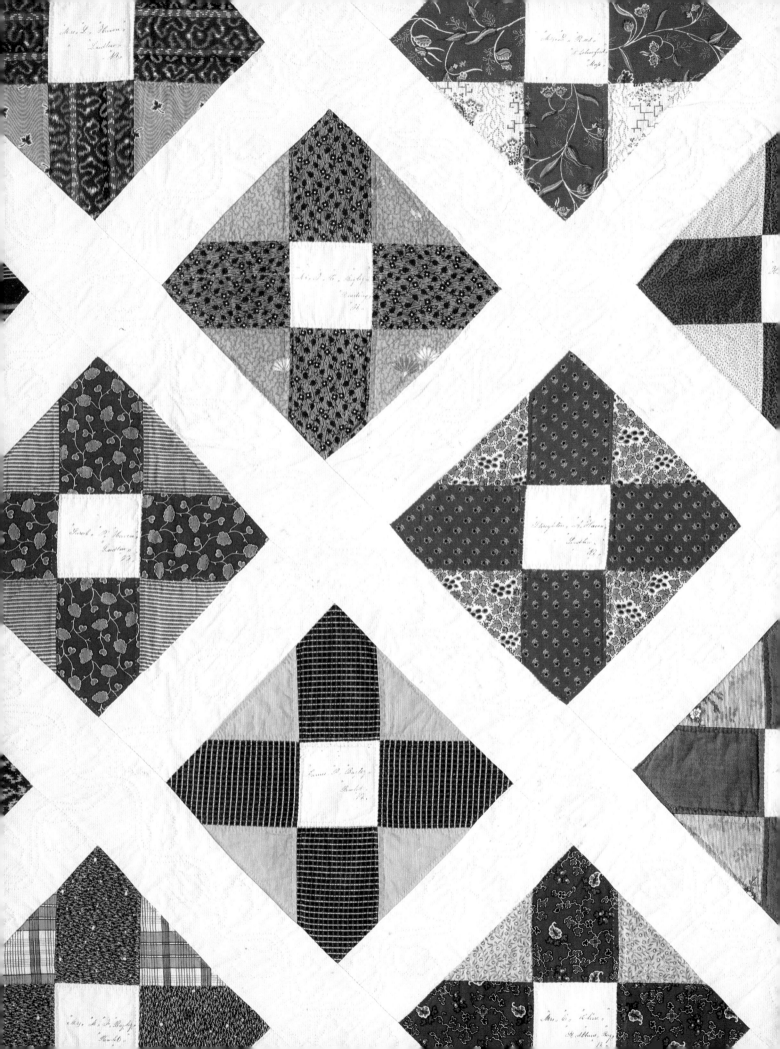

Album Patch, *by Leonora Spaulding Bagley, Ludlow, Vermont, 1854,*
91 × 96 inches, pieced cottons and hand-painted chintz.

A Piece of Ellen's Dress

In
the summer of
1854, inside an enormous
four-story brick house at the corner
of Main and Andover in Ludlow, Vermont,
Ella-Elizabeth Spaulding joyously prepared for her
approaching wedding and move west. Ellen, as she was called
by all her friends and family, thought back to those exciting spring days
several months earlier, when her first cousin Willard Reed had
come from his home in Chelmsford, Massachusetts, to ask for
her hand in marriage. She had known him for as long as
she could remember, from his family's visits to the
Spauldings. But Ellen had never known
him to be so happy or enthusiastic
as he was now at twenty-one,
with all his plans and
dreams of getting
rich in the
West.

A late-nineteenth-century photograph of the Spaulding home, with its attached gristmill, where Ellen grew up in Ludlow, Vermont. Courtesy of Barbara Chiolino.

He had always seemed too serious, hard-working, sometimes even melancholy, and understandably so, as he had experienced frequent tragedies since a little boy. There had been so much sadness. When he was two, his mother, Leonora Spaulding Reed, had died. His father, Joseph Reed, had quickly married Maria Eaton, and then during his childhood six of his tiny half brothers and sisters had died. It was no wonder to Ellen that Willard had developed his persistent, deep-seated belief that he was "no favored child of fortune."[1]

In contrast, except for the death of her grandmother Rhoda White Spaulding in 1848, Ellen could look back on a gregarious, carefree life. Naïve, even somewhat spoiled, but always fun-loving and witty, she

would be an appropriate complement to Willard.

As Ellen sat cross-stitching her initials into a finely woven cotton pillowcase, she envisioned Willard fifteen hundred miles west in Burke, Dane County, Wisconsin, building her a house and preparing for their life together. She imagined land as far as she could see — their land — and an impressive, large home in the "best of society."[2] She would be dressed in the latest fashions, and every day have ladies to tea in her own elegant home. The words printed on her calling card were symbolic of Ellen at this time in her life:

Cheerful singing, Lively measure,
 voices ringing, joy and pleasure
Lengthen out the happy day,
 Lengthen out the happy day.

Ellen was overjoyed. Willard had promised to return for her within several months. They would then be married and start their home together in Burke. Her new life would be full of excitement and adventure. Indeed, she had no fear now that she would be an old maid: she was going to be one of the first among her friends to marry.

But her only sister Leonora and her mother, father and grandparents, although happy for Ellen and her bright future, were sickened at the thought of her leaving and the many miles that would separate them. To ease their pain, they each made promises and plans to move to Burke soon. In the meantime, all of them wished to send something of themselves with her, a special heirloom for Ellen to keep and to remember them by. It was then that Leonora conceived of the friendship quilt. There could be no more loving, precious gift for Leonora to give her four-year-younger sister. And Leonora, her third child due in August, needed a project to keep her hands busy.

Making quilts was second nature to Leonora and Ellen, as to all the women of the Spaulding family. Their needlework skills had been passed on since their ancestor Susanna White had arrived on the *Mayflower*. Those early settlers had been forced through necessity to be self-sufficient. They had to plant flax, spin, weave and dye their own cloth, then construct their clothing. As generations passed, the Spauldings and Whites began buying some imported cloth. A receipt of February 7, 1802, from Concord, New Hampshire, records that Asa Spaulding, Leonora and Ellen's grandfather, "Bo't of John White At his Variety Store, where may be had a large assortment of English and West India GOODS," indigo, copperas and logwood dyes for their homespun, but also "3/4 yard India Cotton."

Within three more generations, spinning, weaving and dyeing cloth had become unnecessary and forgotten skills in the Spaulding family. The family could buy all the cloth they needed, so Ellen and Leonora grew up wearing dresses of fine printed cottons, silks, lawns and delaines made by their mother Arterista and grandmother Lydia Haven. The use of the needle continued to be one of their most important and necessary skills.

But now necessity joined with another aspect of needlework in America — the great pride and even vanity of fine stitches and the final creation. America's quilts reflected this: from coarsely made, home-dyed linsey-woolseys during hard times to elegant, exquisitely stitched red and green appliqués, and all-white "best" quilts during periods of comfort. Thus, the purpose of Leonora's friendship quilt was for warmth and comfort, but not just physically: it was for the warmth and comfort of the soul.

Leonora and Ellen were not without skills of the needle. Like all girls of the time, they held the delicate tool in their tiny, clumsy

fingers by four years of age, piecing together simple four-patch blocks of sprigged and flowered calicoes. They had helped thread needles while the women and older girls put their finest stitches into Grandma's latest patchwork quilt. Both girls held fond memories of the fun of a quilting. Later, what pride they had taken in being invited to sit at the frame and add their best work. The family news and gossip of the community melted the hours away — hours that formed an integral part of their upbringing.

Soon Leonora and then Ellen were preparing for the day when they each would be "keeping house." They followed the tradition of cross-stitching their initials and numbering each of their already carefully hand-hemmed sheets and pillowcases. Leonora stitched one set in minuscule cross-stitch with fine bronze-colored silk thread. She used the lettering she had learned when making her sampler in school and recorded $^{L.A.S}_{6}$ on each of the pillowcases. Leonora and Ellen also pieced many quilt tops for their hope chests. And before their weddings there would be "great quilt-

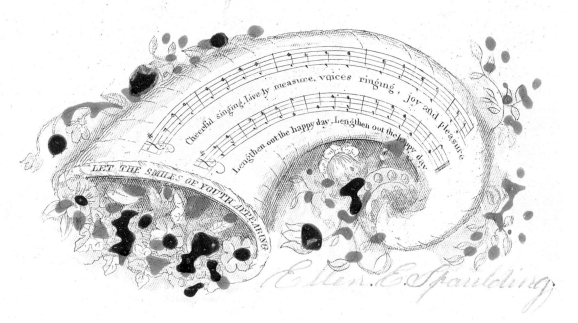

Ellen's hand-painted calling card. Courtesy of Barbara Chiolino.

ings" to transform the one-dimensional, lifeless patchwork tops magically into useful, artistic, living heirlooms.

*B*y the spring of 1854, that period of Leonora's life was only a treasured memory. Thomas Bagley and she had been married in January 1849, when she was only seventeen. Now she had two boys and was pregnant again. Her busy life and her husband's financial difficulties had begun to show in her appearance, although she was not yet twenty-two years of age. But Leonora and her family had recently moved from their home in Reading, Vermont, into her parents' spacious brick home in Ludlow. She now had Ellen and her mother to help with the boys, and more time for her sewing and herself. She quickly became caught up in Ellen's exuberance and her own preparations for the wedding/going-away present.

Unlike the usual fashion of each participating friend making a block, signing it, then returning it to the person assembling the top, Leonora began collecting pieces of printed cottons, the cuttings of shirts and dresses of family and friends; she needed two co-ordinating fabrics for each block. The family was large, and there were also many friends and neighbors who should be included. The list grew to sixty-four: this would have to be a large quilt, with so many nine-inch

A late-nineteenth-century photograph of Ludlow, Vermont, with the Spaulding home near the center. Courtesy of Barbara Chiolino.

blocks. Leonora had chosen the *Album Patch* pattern for Ellen's quilt, and began piecing the blocks with precision. She pieced her father's block from scraps her mother had saved of his clothing. Ellen's block was pieced of scraps of two of Ellen's new dresses, one of large maroon roses and rosebuds on stems, the other a soft rose, small-print calico. Every block was meaningful. Then Leonora made several blocks that were loving memorials to deceased family members: there was their grandmother Rhoda White Spaulding, and Leonora had to include Willard's mother, Leonora Spaulding Reed, who had died in 1835 at only twenty-six years of age. Hers was a special block pieced of imported, madder-dyed, hand-painted Indian cotton.

After her completion of the blocks, Leonora did not ask the sixty-four individuals to sign them, since cloth was difficult to write upon. A mistake, blob of ink or unclear signature would spoil the block, so Leonora had one person with fine penmanship (whose identity is unknown) record the name, town and state on each block. Then she set the blocks together on the diagonal with 3¼-inch sashing between them. Within several months, the top was completed and ready to be quilted. But Leonora needed a large backing. Yardage of muslin, printed cotton or longcloth (coarse, American-manufactured cotton resembling homespun) normally would have been used, but that would have been expensive and not nearly as meaningful as Leonora's choice. She used her own cross-stitch-initialed linens, one darned cotton sheet and a pair of pillowcases, those that she had joyously stitched for her own hope chest years earlier. Then the backing was set in the frame, a thin cotton batt spread evenly on top of that, and

finally the top. And then there was another quilting.

*T*he months passed quickly and, without a letter of warning, Ellen's fiancé appeared at the Spaulding doorstep in Ludlow at the end of August or early in September. The Spaulding household was in a state of uproar: nothing but the quilt was ready for the trip to Wisconsin. Ellen's father had left for Burke, Wisconsin, looking over where his daughter would be living. Willard and he had unknowingly passed each other in their travels. Ellen was not packed. But Willard was impatient; his neighbors in Burke were caring for his livestock and fields, and cold weather might set in soon. The family pulled themselves together, and on September 5, 1854, nineteen-year-old Ella-Elizabeth Spaulding was married to Joseph Willard Reed. After-

wards, Ellen was presented her wedding/going-away present—Leonora's friendship quilt.

Willard believed in traveling light at the cost of practicality. He advised Ellen to take only the clothes she needed, and to have her mother send everything else. Besides a trunk of necessities, Ellen decided to take her "banbox" containing a green bonnet and another bonnet with trimmings.[3] And, of course, Ellen could not leave behind her only keepsake, the cloth album of her family and friends. The quilt was her link with all that she was leaving. The quilts and linens she had sewn for her hope chest she packed to be sent later.

After four exhausting, bone-jarring days and nights on stages, trains, a steamboat and rigs, Ellen and Willard arrived in Burke on September 10. The next morning, she wrote to her mother and father that she and Willard "had a very

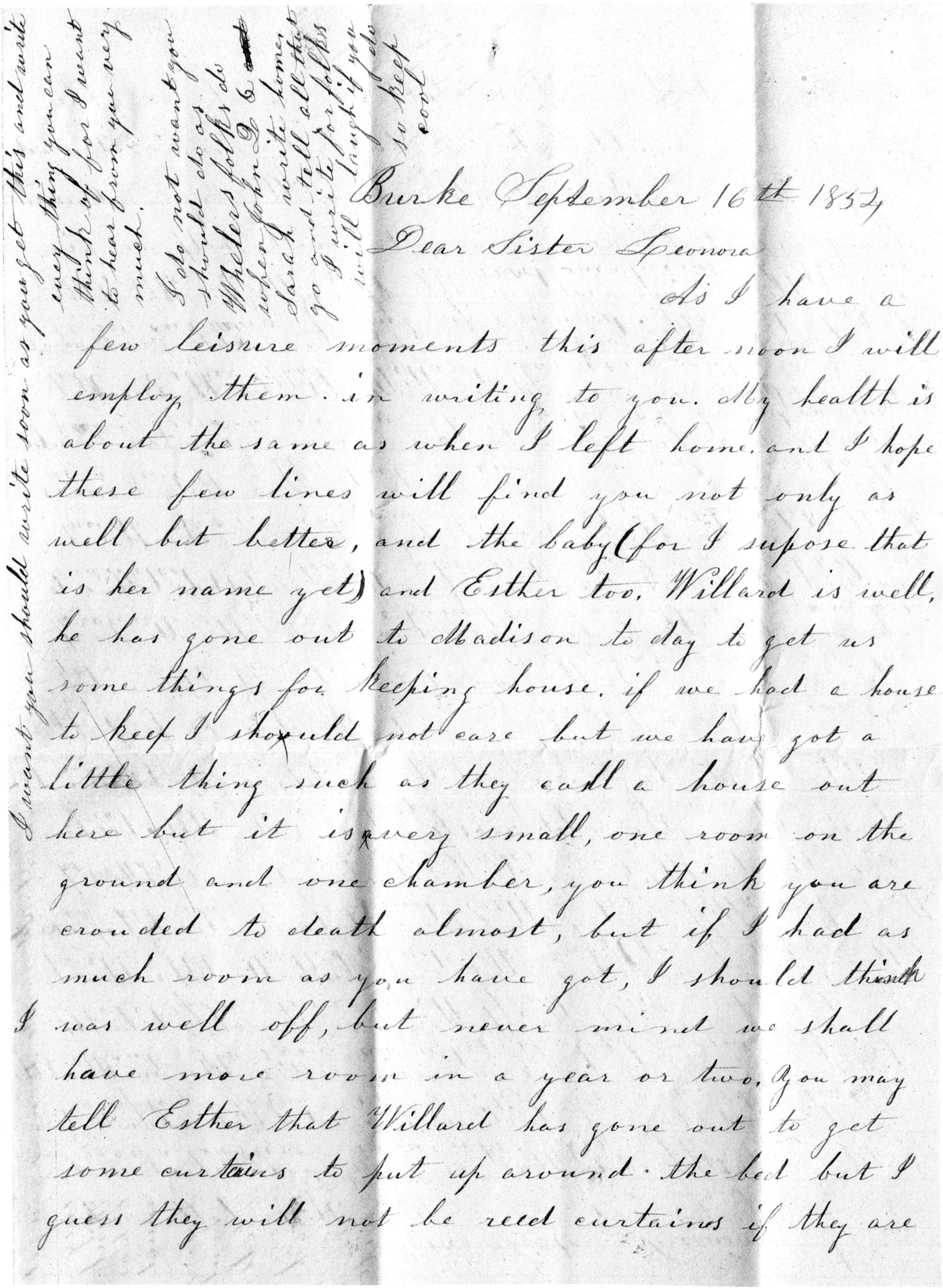

Burke September 16th 1854

Dear Sister Leonora

As I have a few leisure moments this after noon I will employ them in writing to you. My health is about the same as when I left home. and I hope these few lines will find you not only as well but better, and the baby (for I supose that is her name yet) and Esther too. Willard is well, he has gone out to Madison to day to get us some things for keeping house. if we had a house to keep I should not care but we have got a little thing such as they call a house out here but it is very small, one room on the ground and one chamber, you think you are crouded to death almost, but if I had as much room as you have got, I should think I was well off, but never mind we shall have more room in a year or two, You may tell Esther that Willard has gone out to get some curtains to put up around the bed but I guess they will not be reed curtains if they are

I want you should write soon as you get this and write every thing you can think of for I want to hear from you very much.

I do not want you should do as the rest of the folks do when folks do when John & Sarah write home, go and tell all that I write for folks to laugh if you will so keep cool

Ellen's letter to Leonora, September 16, 1854. Courtesy of Barbara Chiolino.

pleasent time and got along well," and that her things "come safe all but the banbox and that got wet and smashed so that [her] green bonnet is spoiled and the other one wet a little." [3] But, all in all, she sounded happy with her new life and her husband's choice of land. She bragged to her parents, "I think it is as good looking place here as I have seen any where on the road and it will laugh well at the old Vermont hills and rocks in a few years when there is some good houses built for that is all that is lacking here." [3]

For several days they lived with Dolly and Abner Cady and their children in the large, two-story brick house across Portage Road from Willard's land: "We are going to stay here a few days untill we get things straitned at home and then we are going to living. the folks here look and act odd to me but they are good and very accomodading to us." [3] Then the newlyweds moved into their own home. Ellen was extremely disappointed and wrote to her sister, "we have got a little thing such as they call a house out here but it is very small, one room on the ground and one chamber, you think you are crouded to death almost, but if I had as much room as you have got, I should think I was well off." [4]

So Ellen worked in her tiny cabin, while Willard was off plowing. She washed the wooden ware from breakfast; then, in her words, "I raked up my fire soon as I got my breakfast out of the way and am sitting with the door open and am warm enough for comfort." [5] She finished her letter. Then silence. Nothingness. No one to talk to — but herself. In the distance there was the crack and deep thud of a falling tree. Ellen dwelt alone from dawn until supper. On September

Leonora's initials with number on the cotton sheet used as a portion of the backing.

16, one week after her arrival in Burke, Ellen wrote, "I have washed ironed and churned this weeke I guess you would laugh to see my great plate of butter but I did not commence setting the milk till Tuesday and churned last night [Saturday] and I got about two lbs. of butter and that is pretty well is it not for two cows <u>and one of them with a bell on her neck</u>." [4]

She also cooked meat and potatoes and baked huge loaves of wheat bread and small biscuits for tea. Her explanation of cooking in the West was, "and now I suppose you will ask when I baked, the folks do not have any sellars out this way, or at least we have not any so we live city fashion cook enough for one meel and let the next one take care of its self." [4] In addition, Ellen made cheese, fed the chickens, milked the cows, straightened her cabin, knitted stockings and sewed plainwaisted dresses for herself and shirts for Willard. It would seem she would not have time for loneliness, but one week after her arrival in Wisconsin, she wrote to her sis-

ter, "I suppose you are all guessing by this time that I am homesick but I am not for I can eat drink and sleep and folks say they can't when they are homesick but I am lonely when Willard is gone, he has been gone one other day this week a threshing for a man that he owed a days work and I expect he has got to go one day next week to work for a man on the marsh." [4] She did have one visitor that week: "There was a Norwegean woman came here this morning after Willard went away and I could not understand hardly a word she said but at last I found out that it was a pig that she wanted so I went out with her and helped catch it and then she carried it off in her dress before real Paddy style." [4]

The lonely days seemed endless to Ellen. Weeks slowly passed without visitors, the complete opposite of her life in Vermont. Thinking back, she could not remember being alone for even one day. Her family was so large, and most of them lived within a few miles. Grandma Haven lived right around the corner, and Ellen could walk over there and help Grandma piece or quilt any time she wanted. And what Ellen would have given to visit just one of her numerous school friends. Her mother and father had warned her she would be lonely out west. Ellen had almost laughed. But then, what had she known of loneliness? Now her only conversations with other women were through letters. Letters were exchanged between Ellen and her mother and sister with two-week-old gossip and news. Occasionally, the envelopes would be thicker than usual; those were exciting ones. There were no instant photos, only fragile, expensive daguerreotypes. Besides these, the handwritten word, handmade diagrams, checks and money orders were usually all that were sent in envelopes—except for cloth. The women sent pieces of their new dresses or comforters and a drawing or pattern to illustrate the style. These pretty scraps of bright calicoes transported Ellen home for a few moments. She could envision Leonora's new dress and also include that piece in her new quilt. And back in Ludlow, Leonora and Arterista and Grandma Haven prized their pieces of Ellen's new dress or Willard's shirt. After all, these pieces were from "the far West." Never were they returned to their envelopes. The family read and re-read the letters, then put them carefully back into the envelopes and saved them, but the pieces of cloth were used. These pieces of their loved ones' clothing were sewn together into precious blocks for their quilts, and were their most tangible ties to each other.

Ellen had pieced blocks and quilted since she could remember. Quilting was an integral part of her life. She was comfortable and happy at a quilting frame and now, in Wisconsin, certainly missed quilting with her grandmother and the other women in the family. Through her correspondence, her mother would describe what Grandma was making, but that only made Ellen more lonely—homesick, actually, but Ellen refused to call it that.

Six painful weeks had ended. Ellen wrote she had "not been a visiting yet nor had company but once Mrs Cady came and spent one afternoon." But then Ellen had some relieving news for her mother: "I have been and helped her [Mrs. Cady] quilt two afternoons she had a great quilting there was a lot of the neighbors there and some of them spoke to me and some went home without as much as saying why do you so (as Uncle Alden said) I expect they were affraid they should get bit."[5]

In Ellen's life in Wisconsin, that quilting at the Cadys' was her only big social event. Willard and she did not attend church services at the log school or neighbors' homes, and Ellen never mentioned actually attending a wedding or funeral, only that so-and-so had been married or died. Except on a Sunday, Willard was most likely too busy to take her. It was only a nearby quilting bee to which Ellen could go without him. Unfortunately for Ellen, within days of the quilting, the Cadys left for better virgin farmland, government land in Iowa. With Mrs. Cady went her "great quiltings."

As the plow and axe were Willard's companions in the West, the needle and pen were Ellen's. They were her means of survival, her companions in her hours of severe loneliness and depression, while her husband was away working. She tried to keep herself busy with needlework after completing her

other household duties. In spite of solitude, she found contentment in her accomplishments: "I am footing a pair of stockings for myself now, ... and have made Willard a pair of pants and he fetched home cloth for another pair last night, so you see I am jack at all traids."[6] And besides all of her other sewing, she was also piecing quilts. She wrote on March 19, 1856, "I am pieceing me a comfortable, called Boneparts retreat."[7]

Ellen grew more and more intensely homesick and longed to be a part of her family's get-togethers, especially the quiltings. Her mother was beginning a comfortable and sent Ellen a piece. In another letter Ellen wrote, "I think your dress and aprons very pretty, and Grandmas quilt." Ellen deeply meant it when she added, "I wish I could come and help her quilt it."[8]

There was no hope of a quilting invitation in the West for Ellen now. Willard had grown dissatisfied and moved her to virgin land with more wood and water, about eighty-five miles northwest in Glendale Township, Juneau County, Wisconsin. Once again her husband was engulfed in clearing, grubbing, breaking and fencing, leaving Ellen from dawn until dusk to occupy herself. The nearest town was Mauston, sixteen miles away, but the supplies there were limited. Willard had to go nearly a hundred miles back to Madison for a good selection of calico and other printed cottons for Ellen's new dresses and quilts. And Ellen always wrote home proudly about a new dress and sent a piece for her mother and grandmother. Each piece of cloth now became precious to Ellen. She had to wait months for Willard to surprise her with more. Besides, even the purchase of cloth was a sacrifice to them now that there were such "hard times"[9] throughout the western country. Ellen was

Memorial block for Willard's mother,
Leonora Spaulding Reed, made with an Indian madder-dyed, hand-painted chintz.

forced to make her tiny scraps last. She began piecing blocks for another quilt.

But the depression of 1857 had much more serious results than a shortage of cloth for Ellen and Willard. There was a severe shortage of food and other material necessities. "Money is very scarce out here, and all kinds of grain is down low and every thing we have to buy is very high and we can not get trusted to the stores any, (and I am glad of that), so we can live without....we have not had any meat lately, nor a speck of butter for weeks and weeks, there is none in the country to be bought, so there it is again, and we cant get a cow till we get some money so we live on potatoe and salt with a little milk on it, and bread without but-

ter, and have lived weeks this summer without a speck of sugar in the house, and have three or four ladies some out from Mauston, and nothing for tea but biscuit and a little butter I had some then and tea, but that is nothing it is out wist in the land that flows with milk and honey."[9]

No longer was Ellen immature or naïve. The three years in the West had forced her to grow up quickly and to perceive life in a serious vein. And Ellen was also brave. For several years she had continued to go about as normally as she could with a "hard cough." But with her poor diet and loneliness resulting in deep depression, her condition had continually grown worse, and she wrote, "My health has been very poor ever since I came out here [Glendale] last fall, and I do not think it is much better nor looks very incourageing for me. I have a very hard cough all of the time, and have had hard colds one after the other all summer and fall. I am takeing Wisters Balsom of wild Cherry and think it helps me some, and would a great deel more if I had half a chance for my life, but you think it is hard times there where you have enough of every thing, but I guess if you was out here as we, and thousands of others have been, you would not call that hard, but we have been obliged to live so because we could not get our money for things that we sold nor where it was due us."[9]

In spite of her poor, fragile condition, Ellen had not forgotten to include another swatch of cotton in

"Wisters Balsom of wild Cherry."

a letter two weeks earlier: "that piece I sent you in his [Willard's] letter was a piece of my new dress." And she continued, "I have got my knitting and sewing most done, I have done my work with what Willard helps me, all but my washing. I have not washed a thing but twice since early last spring, and you need not think it is the seven nor nine month consumption that ails me either, if you do you are mistaken."[9]

In April 1858, after nearly four years of Ellen's invitations and pleading, her parents finally arrived at their children's newly completed two-story "house made of Popple logs"[9] in Glendale Township, Wisconsin. Stedman and Arterista, unsuspecting of the seriousness of

"It is a very lonely place I think, not near so pleasant as it was down to Burke" was how Ellen described, in a letter to her parents, this river valley which could be seen from the window of her "house made of Popple logs" in Glendale, Wisconsin.

Ellen's illness, were shocked by their daughter's emaciated body, her critical state.

For three months they nursed her. Her compassionate father "mooved her from one bed to the other"[10] several times in the day, trying to make her more comfortable. Stedman wrote that "Ellen had sustained the idea that her disorder was not the consumption and that she should get better by and by and be able to return to Vermont with us next fall or winter which She ever expressed considerable anxiety for doing. and when her flesh and strength was so gone that she could not set in her chair nor bear her weight on her feet she thought still that she would start to go home if we would go with her, but the Doctor said her lungs were so much deceyed that the moment we went to mooving her they would break down and she would certainly die."[10]

Despite her family's loving care and companionship, Ellen's death was inevitable, and "she breathed out her last gust, Monday Eight-Oclock in the after noon,"[10] July 12, 1858, one month before her twenty-third birthday.

When Ellen Reed died, she did not have many possessions, and fewer still of value from her dour

Ellen's gravestone, Ludlow, Vermont.

ROBERT LIPSETT

western existence. There were only some personal articles and her quilts. Upon her deathbed, she asked her parents to give those quilts to members of the family. Nearly two years after her death, Willard's father thanked Stedman and Arterista Spaulding: "Ellens quilts came safe and were very gladly receivd by us and also Charles and Emily rec'd thiers with great pleasure." Then Maria Reed added, "we received Ellens kind

presant and feel very much pleased with them and feell very greatful to you for your trouble and hope I can repay you someetime."[11]

And Ellen's wedding gift from her sister, her cherished friendship quilt, was returned to her sister.

There was one more request Ellen made of her parents. When she had accepted her fast-approaching death, Ellen requested they "take her remains back to Ludlow."[10] So on April 18, 1859, nine months after her death, Ellen's body was finally laid to rest in the quiet, secluded cemetery on the hill, only one long block from her family's home in Ludlow, Vermont.

While still in Glendale, Wisconsin, Ellen's father had written to Leonora, "I hope they [his grandchildren] will all of them remember her so that she will not be forgotten by them."[12] One hundred and twenty-seven years have passed since Stedman's letter to Leonora. The brick home at the corner of Main and Andover is gone; a post office stands in its place. Willard's years of toil in constructing log houses, barns and rail fences have slowly been erased from the Wisconsin landscape. Only the letters and Ellen's friendship quilt survive so we can relive Ellen's story and see a piece of Ellen's dress.

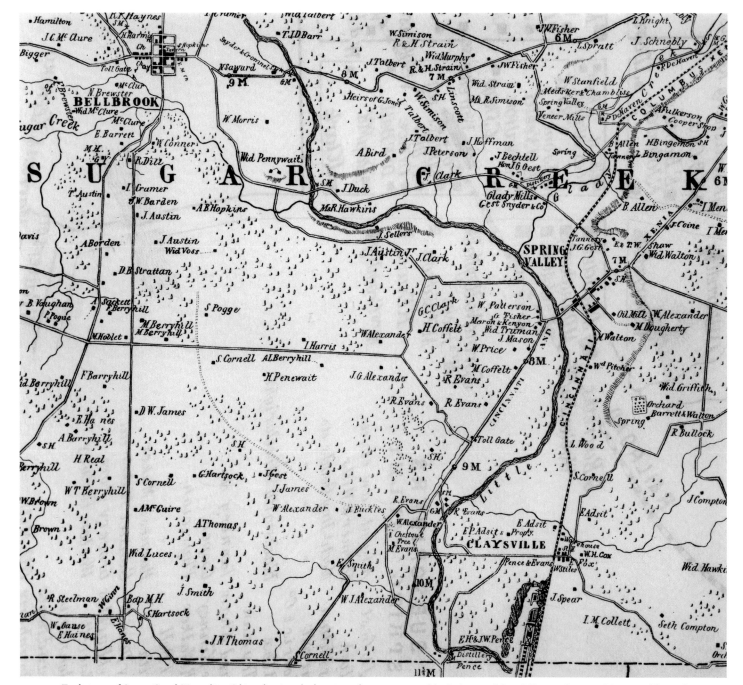

Early map of Sugar Creek Township, Ohio, showing the location of property owned by Robert and Sarah Evans, their son Moses and his wife Sarah S. and many relatives and neighbors. (Robert's gristmill, for example, is marked "GM" near the Little Miami River on the map.) Many of these neighbors and relatives gave Sarah S. blocks for her quilt. From 1855 Atlas from the Map of Greene County, Ohio.

Two Pair
Quilting Frames

*L*ong
ago, in a green, shady Ohio valley, there were
two Sarah Evanses, two Quaker houses,
two large families and two quilting
frames. Even though their
names were the same,
these two Sarahs
were very dif-
ferent — in
age, in appear-
ance, in personality. Yet
their lives became inter-
woven in the mid-nineteenth century as mother-in-law and daughter-
in-law. So intertwined were they that the
two Sarah Evanses became fused in memories

*Family composite of Robert and Sarah Evans, six of their children (inner circle) and eighteen of their grandchildren (outer circle).
In the inner circle is Moses, husband of Sarah S., and on the right side of the outer circle is Robert, their son, in his Civil War uniform.
Courtesy of Elizabeth Josephine Evans Brown, a great-granddaughter of Sarah S.*

as one—or perhaps the first Sarah was completely forgotten. Nevertheless, each Sarah made a quilt that is not forgotten, and each quilt is signed differently—"Sarah Evans" and "Sarah S. Evans"—that the makers should not be confused.

Sarah Evans was fifty-five years old when she quilted "Sarah Evans 1854" into the left-hand corner of her completed *Whig Rose* quilt, and Sarah S. Evans only in her early thirties when she wrote "Sarah S. Evans" onto two blocks for her friendship quilt. Already these two Sarahs' lives were pieced together as the patchwork in their quilting frames. But it had not always been so. There had been a time when there was only one Sarah Evans in that peaceful valley in western Ohio....

Sarah Coppock Evans was thirty years old, her eldest child eleven, one in arms and many in-between on that Thursday, September 24, 1829, when the family was ready to leave Newberry District, South Carolina, for their new home in Greene County, Ohio. Sarah was exhausted. She had toiled for weeks, preparing for this journey; she had only the covered wagon for her babies, the older children and most of their belongings. So many precious items she had to leave behind. Yet all of her Quaker neighbors were in the same situation. In fact, almost the entire Society of Friends of Newberry had already left or were making plans to leave for Ohio. Their firm religious beliefs would not allow them to remain in South Carolina—at least, not as long as their neighbors on nearby plantations owned slaves.

Sarah could bring only a few fragile keepsakes. Most of the space in the wagon had to be saved for sleeping, with lots of quilts and bedding packed, and there had to be room for all the food they would need for one month. She could not fill the space with the prized possessions left to her by a loving, departed mother, and from twelve years of marriage. Leaving was not as difficult for Robert, her husband. His Quaker mother and stepfather

Early photograph of Ohio Quakers, found among Sarah S.'s personal keepsakes.

had left for Ohio three years earlier, so Robert had a temporary home for his family on the other side of the mountains, only one month away. And he planned to begin again his gristmill business in Ohio.

Thirty-one days later, the family did indeed stop their four-horse team and one-horse wagon in front of the Speerses' log house in Sugar Creek, Greene County, Ohio, after a tiring, uncomfortable but safe journey through the Cumberland Pass by way of the Wilderness Road and old Warrior Path to Ohio.[1]

Robert Evans immediately secured four hundred acres of heavily wooded land on the west side of the Little Miami River and, armed with only an axe, began clearing a small space within the dense, dark forest for his log house and a few crops. But quickly winter had set in to an extreme unknown to these Southerners and, their cabin not yet completed, they had to share the Speerses' house until spring.[2]

By summer, Sarah was adjusting to her hewn log house within the verdant, thick woods, the clear Little Miami River meandering through. And, as she nursed her baby, amidst laughter and shrieks of children of all ages, she could hear explosive cracks followed by the reverberating thud of a tree crashing onto the forest floor. Sarah did not see much of her husband when the weather was tolerable. He was far off, clearing another acre of forest, or along the river south of the log house, erecting his saw and gristmills. Robert Evans was industrious and, within a scant five years, water was perpetually splashing over his huge wooden wheels, providing power for grinding corn and wheat and for sawing felled trees into plank boards for new, more civilized houses.

Sarah's husband toiled long hours every day, except for meeting days and the Sabbath. But Sarah's days were longer, and she had no days of rest, taking care of many little ones, along with all of a woman's other responsibilities. Her husband had built their house, raised their food and chopped their wood, yet the family's survival was equally on Sarah's shoulders. It was up to her to nourish her family, and from the work of her hands to clothe them and keep them warm, to heal them when sick, and to provide most of the household necessities such as soap, dipped candles, even fire in the hearth. Unlike her husband's, Sarah's work did not cease with the sunset, or in the quiet, long hours of the night when the wind howled through the cracks of the chinking as she nursed a sick child or hungry infant. She might be many months pregnant or weak from childbirth, or distraught over the death of her infant or child; nevertheless, Sarah could not rest: she must work yet another day.

In all, from the time she was twenty until in her early forties, Sarah was pregnant fifteen times, and in childbirth fifteen times, and many of these infants were born there in Ohio. Sarah was a strong Quaker woman, but some of her fifteen babies were not so strong. Two of her infants did not survive, in spite of Sarah's fight to save them. And four of her children died over the years when seasonal diseases swept through the valley. They were buried in little graves nearby.

Of the nine children who lived, there were only two boys, Moses and Isaac, eventually to help their tired father; the rest were girls (Rebecca, Esther, Lydia, Mary, Sophia, Nancy J. and Margaret E.). Robert Evans would have liked to have more help on his farm and in the mills but, instead, there were seven girls in the house. And Sarah began teaching her girls the things women needed to know: to piece blocks for warm quilts and to sew a fine seam as soon as their small fingers were able to co-ordinate a needle, to spin and weave, to knit. And the girls helped their mother with the new baby and the toddlers, as well as in the kitchen and garden.

But Sarah's children were growing up. In 1842, thirteen years after her arrival in Ohio, Sarah had children ranging in age from three to twenty-four. Sarah and Robert had prospered in this new state. They lived in a comfortable, but simply furnished, plank house surrounded by their fertile, plowed fields, and the R. Evans & Sons Mills along the river operated daily, except for the days of their meetings: Fifth-day (Thursday) weekly, Seventh-day (Saturday) monthly and every First-day (Sunday) at eleven. On those days, the large Evans family would separate at the double doors of the log Caesar's Creek meeting house. Robert, in a drab suit and a broad-brimmed beaver hat,[3] would lead his sons to the men's unpainted wooden benches through the right-

hand door and Sarah and the girls would open the left-hand door to the women's side. There, Sarah and the girls, in white muslin caps, plain stiff bonnets and simple, quiet-colored dresses, "sat covered and in silence for an hour, unless the spirit moved some Friend to speak."[4] There was "no bell, no organ, no choir, no pulpit, no order of service, no ritual."[5] They each "concentrated on the expectation of divine presence."[6]

Sarah Evans's signature as seen on her quilt (1854) and on a deed (1846) granting land to her son Moses. Deed courtesy of Elizabeth Josephine Evans Brown.

It was at one of these meetings that Sarah S. Evans, then Sarah Shaw Huston, formally entered Sarah Evans's life. At the monthly meeting in February 1842, Sarah's son Moses had announced to the Friends that he wanted to marry another member of the Society, Sarah S. At the March meeting, the Friends had reported them "clear" and "at liberty to accomplish their marriage."[7] So it was on the succeeding Fifth-day, March 24, that Sarah S., standing before the Friends, her right hand placed in Moses' right hand, vowed: "Friends, in the presence of the Lord, and before this assembly, I take this my friend Moses Evans to be my husband; promising, with divine assistance, to be unto him a loving and faithful wife, until death

shall separate us."[8] From that day onward, Sarah Shaw Huston would always be known as Sarah S. Evans. And she would never drop that initial "S." from her signature, for it was very confusing to have two Sarah Evanses within the same family, especially since they would live on farms so near one another.

Sarah S. Evans began quickly to follow her mother-in-law's pattern of a large family. Before she and Moses had been married one year, Sarah S. had already given birth to a baby boy, and named him after his grandfather Robert Evans. By 1854, Moses and Sarah S. were well on their way to their own large family: they already had six children, Robert, Joseph, Daniel, Hannah, Mary Elizabeth and new baby Sophie Angeline ("Angie"). So, like her mother-in-law before her, Sarah S. had her hands full with many small children.

Sarah Evans, however, was fifty-five now and her youngest, Margaret, was fifteen. Finally, after so many years of endless responsibilities, exhausting work, and after the making of so many utilitarian scrap quilts, Sarah Evans had time to make a beautiful appliquéd quilt and, because of her husband's mills down along the Little Miami River, the money to buy factory-made cotton cloth for it. She appliquéd red flowers with pieced centers, green leaves and stems and blue swags to sections of white background. With the top completed and basted to a thin, nearly seedless batt and white backing, Sarah and several of her daughters sat on each side of the large, handmade quilt frame, stitching in one-half-inch diagonal rows. There was only one area in the left-hand corner of the quilt that Sarah asked them to leave unquilted. Into that space of her com-

Whig Rose, by Sarah Evans, Sugar Creek Township, Ohio, 1854, 85 × 81 inches, pieced and appliquéd cottons.

pleted *Whig Rose,* she quilted her signature, "Sarah Evans 1854."

Down the road, Sarah Evans's daughter-in-law Sarah S. was passing on her needlework skills to her young daughters, skills that her mother had learned in South Carolina from her mother before her. When Sarah S. was married, she had brought to their home fine linen sheets and towels she had woven, hand-hemmed and signed, as well as quilts she had made. And she wanted her daughters to do the same, so that they would be good wives.

In 1858, Sarah S. was collecting blocks for a special quilt, not an appliquéd one like her mother-in-law's, but a simple, pieced friendship quilt. Sarah S. had seven children now, her youngest son (Hillie) only a year, her eldest (Robert) nearly sixteen. Her Quaker friends, sisters-in-law and other Evans relatives were each making a block, signing it and returning the block to Sarah S. The process was slow: it took two years for her to collect all the blocks, each with a different fabric, for her quilt top. But in 1860, Sarah S. had a quilting for her neighbors, friends and sisters-in-law, and the forty-nine seven-inch blocks were transformed into a lovely heirloom.

By the time Sarah S. Evans's friendship quilt was completed, her sisters-in-law were nearly all mar-

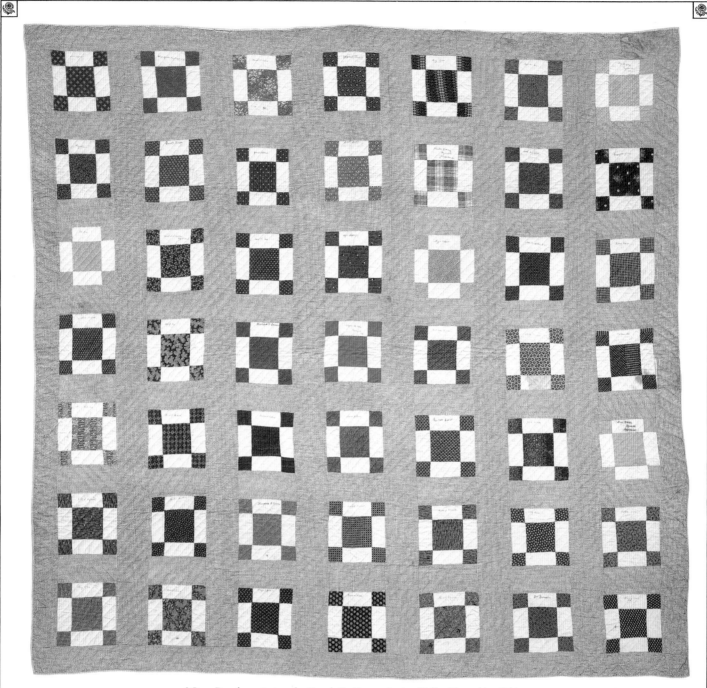

Nine Patch *variation, by Sarah S. Evans, Spring Valley Township, Ohio,*
1858–1860, 83 × 79 inches, pieced cottons.

ried and living in homes of their own. Their names were changed to Esther Hartsock, Mary Barrett, Sophia Whitney, Nancy J. Peterson and Margaret E. Babbs (later Mrs. Aaron Crites). And most of them lived there in Spring Valley (formerly Sugar Creek) Township. Even Sarah S.'s brother-in-law Isaac Evans married the year her quilt was completed (1860), but he continued to take care of the books for his father's mills.

The Evans families' farms and mills were prospering there on the Little Miami, and they were one large, happy family. But on April 12, 1861, Fort Sumter was fired upon and war had begun — the war between the North, and the South where their Quaker ancestors had "stayed quietly"[9] over one hundred years, the South from which Sarah, Robert, Moses Evans and Sarah S.'s parents, the Hustons, had migrated because of the evils of slavery. And now their Quaker sons were expected to fight against those they had quietly and peacefully left. For Sarah S. Evans, the war could not have come at a worse time, for she had two sons of age, Robert (eighteen) and Joseph (sixteen),

92

and she was expecting her eighth child.

At first, to Sarah S.'s relief, there were plenty of volunteers, but the battles and years pushed onward. Her boys were Quakers from birth; their grandparents and great-grandparents were all Quakers before them. They were men of peace with a firm inborn opposition to fighting; yet the Evanses, like many of their Quaker neighbors, were passionate abolitionists and supporters of the Union.[10] "The abolition of slavery [was] more important [to them] than the evils of war."[11] And, with the new draft law in March of 1863, Sarah S. and Moses' two sons felt pressure to enlist with their friends before being drafted.

Soon Joseph and Robert both were in uniform, Joseph only in the hundred-days' service, but Robert enlisted in August of 1863 and was mustered into Company H, Second Ohio Volunteer Heavy Artillery, in September of that year. A few months later, Sarah S. became

alarmed to learn that Robert was in a hospital with a severe case of smallpox. It was such a relief to hear from him in June and to know that he was better:

Photograph of Robert Evans, enlarged from his paternal grandparents' family composite.

Munfordsville June 22nd
Dear Mother.
    I received your kind letter a few days scince and was pleased to hear from you and to hear that you were

all well   I am well and hearty.   there is not very many here that are sick at present   Jessie Alexander left here last week   he started for the Regt and I have not heard from him scince   I have not received a letter from T H Boaz for some time   he was well and hearty when he wrote. we have had some very warm weather here for a few days past and the corn needs rain very bad   it will soon be hearvest time   ther wheat will not be very heavy in these parts —
Mother you wished to know where my carpet sack was   it was here at the hospital but my dress coat and one new pair of pants was gone   they were taken before my knapsack and carpet sack were fetched here   Tom told me that he thought he knew who had taken my coat.
you said that if I went south to send my clothes   what I did not need home but be sure and not send any thing that I had about me while sick   I did not fetch a single thing that I had about me away   we had to burn them up   Mother I do not know whesther you would know me or not   my hair has very near all come out ~~but~~ and I am as bald as some old man sixty   I think it will come in again. ~~it has~~   I do not know when I will go to the Regt.   the Doctor says that he intends to have some of us that have had the small posc detailed here to nurse ~~the smal~~   there is none that have that disease now   and I hope there will be no more of it but I will have to close for I fear you will be tired trying to read this   please write soon my love to all
    your affectionate Son,   RH Evans.[12]

*B*ut then Robert had returned to the regiment, and what a severe shock only one year later to be notified from Knoxville, Tennessee, of her son's death from dysentery, July 20, 1865. He had been too weak to recover from that second disease. Adding to her agony, through error, over one year passed before Robert's body was finally sent home and buried in the family plot. Sarah S. cherished the poem

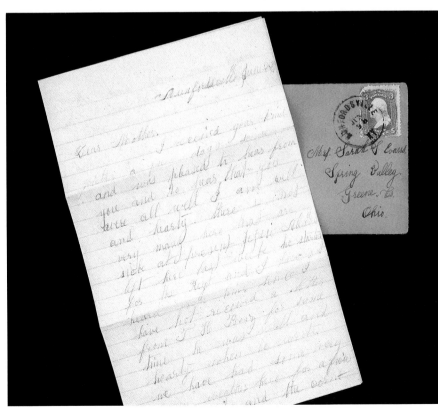

Robert Evans's letter to his mother Sarah S., June 22, 1864.

LINES INSCRIBED
To the Parents of Robert H. Evans,

Who was born Jan. 29th 1843; Volunteered Aug. 12th, 1863, and died July 20th, 1865, aged 22 years, 5 months and 21 days.

The cold earth lies above his form,
 The dark storm of war is past;
But memory can ne'er give up,
 As long as life shall last,
The recollections of our child!
 Our noble, first-born son,
Who gave his life a sacrifice,
 "A young unblemished one."

To save his country from the grasp
 Of treason's treacherous hand,
And shield the homes of loving ones,
 Of his dear native land,—
In the bloom of youth he left us all;
 Bade warm, fond friends adieu;
But once on furlough came again
 The farewells to renew.

A furlough for a last farewell
 To all he held so dear,
To scenes he loved from childhood,
 To sounds he loved to hear,
To all youth's gay companions,
 To tried friends, and true,
To brothers, sisters, parents,
 A fond, long, long adieu.

No more warm hand-clasps here to meet
 Nor loving smiles to know,
Nor sympathizing tones to greet,
 Though the heart be wrung with woe.
And that we are sure has been his lot,
 When affliction pressed him sore,
When small-pox seized upon him,
 Which in loneliness he bore.

And when that last death-sickness
 Came on with fatal power,
And he contemplated quite alone
 The approaching dying hour.
How his young heart yearned for sympathy,

And the fond love at home,
No strong, untried heart can tell;
 Alone with God, alone!

But on the Savior's breast, we trust
 He sweetly did repose,
And in His loving arms did find
 The joys the christian knows;
For we hear he told a comrade,—
 "He was not afraid to die,"
So we trust his pure young spirit
 Ascended home on high,

To dwell forever with the blessed,
 The redeemed from sin and woe,
And the joys of the everlasting life
 In full extent to know.
For though his life was short on earth,
 And though our hearts do mourn,
Yet God is good, and His ways are just,
 And in meekness should be borne.

Now buried three times in the earth,
 His body will repose,
Until the resurrection morn
 All hidden things disclose,
When Christ shall come again on earth,
 To 'waken all that sleep;
Then friends may meet again with
  friends,
 With no more cause to weep.

"Blessed be the name of the Lord
 Who gave and has taken away,"
Blessed all those who in Him trust,
 The sacred Scriptures say;
And blessed are all they that mourn,
 They shall be comforted,
For Christ now pleads for such to God,
 Arisen from the dead.

WRITTEN Sept. 6, 1866.

written in memory of her son for his funeral in September of 1866 (page 94).

Robert's funeral was followed by the deaths of her twenty-year-old son Daniel in the fall of 1868, and then of her own husband, Moses, one month later. Sarah and Robert Evans had been together at the "sittings" (funerals), feeling the losses of their son and grandsons, and they tried to comfort Sarah S.; but only two weeks after Moses' death,

RES. OF SARAH S. EVANS
SPRING VALLEY TP. GREENE CO. O.

on November 9, 1868, Robert Evans himself was dead, and his coffin was lowered into the ground near his children's graves in Woodland Cemetery in Xenia, Ohio. Sarah Evans and Sarah S. Evans quietly wept together, both of them now joined in widowhood and loss.

For Sarah S., however, there was little time to weep. She had to dry her tears and go home; there were too many small children who needed her. At least her now eldest son, twenty-three-year-old Joe, could assume some of his father's responsibilities.

Sarah S. looked out over her husband's fields. These were now hers, *her* responsibility, and Sarah S. added "farmer" to her daily tasks. She guided the oxen as her son plowed, she planted the seed, she reaped the harvest.

Only two and a half years later, when Sarah S. was beginning to adjust to her hard life, her mother-in-law, Sarah Evans, died at seventy-two. Not long after, all of Sarah Evans's belongings were auctioned

off. And with each of those belongings, the whole of that sturdy, staid Quaker woman's life was divided—divided into pieces like the pieces of her quilts, only these pieces would not be stitched together again. They would be scattered about the country over time.

Sarah Evans had made many quilts and linens in her lifetime, most of them utilitarian, for hard use and warmth, but at the auction of her belongings, these were of the highest value.[13] Her "two pr. quilting frames" sold cheap (one to T. S. Houston for 10¢, the other to daughter Margaret for 11¢), but the "bedding" that was quilted in those frames sold at a much higher price than any furniture. One bedstead sold for 6¢, an old dresser for 10¢, and a desk for 50¢, one settee for $1.00, "six Kane bottom chairs" for $6.30, six "Winsor" chairs for $1.68, the buffalo robe $6.45, "1 rock chr. and cush. $5.00." The individual lots of bedding were comparable in value to the sleigh for $10, or the "two horse wagon" for $30. Of the entire inventory list, only the "Buggy" at $100, and the "Eleven Fat Hogs" for $121 were valued more than one group of bedding. All together, however, Sarah's handmade bedding totaled $139.75. That was more than the buggy, and also more than the eleven fat hogs.

Not only was the monetary value higher, Mother's linens, hand-woven blankets and beautiful quilts also had a sentimental value for daughters Margaret, Nancy, Mary and unmarried Rebecca. They bought all but one lot, and that sold to "S. [?]. Evans."

Sarah S. Evans was at her mother-in-law's estate auction. She bought a "lot of dishes" for 35¢, a clothes basket for 60¢ and a tin pan for 15¢, things that her sisters-in-law did not want. But also Sarah S. was careful with her money: she was widowed three years now and had the responsibilities of a farm and five children at home, little Eddie only five years old.

Her situation was difficult, although not unfamiliar. Sarah S.'s own father had died when she was only seven, and her Quaker mother had not remarried but had single-handedly raised Sarah S. and her brother Daniel. Now Sarah S. had no family left nearby. Her mother had died many years earlier, in 1844, and her brother had gone off to California for gold in 1850, returning three years later only to reclaim his wife and children and move them to San Bernardino, California, for good.

Nevertheless, Sarah S. Evans went onward. "She was a big woman and a strong woman,"[14] and she had great faith. She raised her children, plowed and planted her land, and gave thanks for that which she had.

Twelve years after her husband's death, in 1880, her youngest child Eddie was fourteen years old, and five of her seven children still lived at home. Her eldest son, Joe, had married the neighbor girl Anna Buckles, and her daughter Angie was the wife of Newton Berryhill and had a new baby. Both Joe and Angie lived near their mother.

Sarah S.'s youngest daughter, Emma, was nearly nineteen and teaching school several miles away, but she was still able to live at home. Hannah, Hillie or Angie would usually take her in the wagon to the schoolhouse before "½ past 8"[15] in the morning and bring her home in the late afternoons. And Emma would burst into the house with all kinds of conversation about her experiences and daily problems. Later each day she would enter them into her diary: "All the girls wanted to go down and get calimus and I would not let them because I saw them eating in time of school,

I was so provoked, I did not know what to say or do.... One boy run off from school and the girls staid out at recess a long time after school was taken up. that trys a teacher's patients I tell you, if any thing does, so much in one day, or it does mine any how, maybe it don't evry person, I hope not or this would be a terrible world to live in."

The gregarious Evans household was always bustling with activity. There was much work to be done, but many hands to do it. On Saturdays, the girls "swept the parlor,

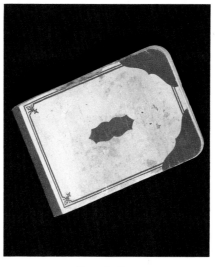

Emma's diary.

cleaned yard, planted beans, scarred the tin things, cleaned the garret, ironed." Sometimes, after their work was completed, the girls went shopping in town: "We did our work, Hannah & I [Emma] went to town in the after noon, got me a hat cost $2.45 shoes $1.80 slippers, real pretty." And later in the day, there was always company or visiting: "Levi Pierson was here for dinner.... Nellie & Jim were over, had lots of fun, did n't go to bed until after 11 I guess." There were also weddings, festivals and funerals in Spring Valley Township.

On Sundays, the family "all went to sunday school and meeting" in the morning, and generally in the

evenings, too. Their meetings, however, were no longer with the Friends; they were now Methodists. "We, Ma, Hannah, Hillie, Eddie & I [Emma] went to S.V. [Spring Valley] to meeting We had a very good meeting no one here to preach, John Daugherty read and others spoke, came home got our dinner.... Hannah, Eddie & I went to Mt Holly to meeting, Mr Carg preached."

Truly, they were a close family and a happy one, but in September of 1881, the Evans household was in deep shock when Emma became ill and died at only twenty years of age, "just as in the morning of her life was opening unto day."[16] Strangely, Emma herself had almost predicted her death in an entry in her diary over a year earlier, when she had written, "Today is the last day of April, oh I wonder where we will all be this time next year, not all together I reckon."

As when her husband and sons had died, Sarah S. Evans suffered at the loss of her "young and lovely"[17] daughter. And as in the sad times of her past, she pushed on. She was a strong woman and proved an indomitable force, always providing a secure, stable, welcome home for her children, family and friends.

But there was a very tender, sentimental side to this big, strong woman and, in quiet moments by herself, she cherished the little keepsakes of her children and earlier years: her son Robert's letter from the Civil War, her daughter Emma's diary, the fine linen wedding sheets —woven, hand-hemmed, signed in ink "Sarah S. Huston. 1842," the year of her marriage—and her friendship quilt made with her Quaker friends. And one more item precious to Sarah S. Evans was the *Whig Rose* quilt appliquéd and quilted a half century before by her mother-in-law, Sarah Evans.

*S*o, along the banks of the Little Miami River in Sugar Creek, Ohio, there were once two pair of quilting frames, two pair of hands, two Sarahs. And many, many quilts did they make.

Sarah S. Evans (seated) with her daughters Angie Berryhill and Mary Elizabeth Evans, c. 1890. Courtesy of Ruth E. Daniel, Sarah S.'s great-granddaughter.

Colleen S. Craft
Born
Sept. 29 1916

Nine Patch *variation, by Julia Stevens Crosby,*
East Hardwick, Vermont, c. 1860, 87 1/2 × 91 inches, pieced cottons.

Julia's Legacy

Julia
wore her home-
spun, empire-waisted frock,
a long woolen apron tied at her waist. Her thick, long brown
hair was stuffed into a white cap covering her head; one of her bare
feet was on the treadle, the other on the plank floor. The crackling crescen-
dos and diminuendos of the glowing hearth and the hum of the flax
wheel kept her company as she spun the fine flax into a long,
even linen thread. Julia wanted this to be her best
work, for she planned to weave
this thread into her
bridal sheets.

Spinning was second nature to Julia, as were most other household tasks. She had begun learning as a small child, standing on an axe-split bench at her mother's side or on the dirt floor of the crude cabin, at her mother's long skirt, ever watching her dipping candlewicks into the bubbling tallow, stirring lye and melted fat for soft soap, soaking tow cloth in the indigo pot. By four years of age, little Julia was already doing safer women's work herself: she was sewing miscellaneous pieces of linen, tow and wool together for warm quilts in the winter, her mother overseeing that she made careful, tiny stitches. And Julia had begun learning early to spin flax and wool and to weave her finished threads into solid, checked or striped fine cloth. But there was nothing unusual about this; all the girls Julia's age in Stevens' Mills and in that part of Vermont could do the same. One could not live otherwise on this northernmost American frontier. These skills were necessary for survival.

This harsh life was all that Julia knew as a child. She had experienced her mother's working through ten pregnancies, she had waited fearfully through ten births, and she had watched her mother's torment and grief after the deaths of two of the infants. Julia had helped raise many of the surviving little ones and she had had many other responsibilities, even as a young girl.

Certainly Julia felt well prepared to begin housekeeping someday soon in her own home. In fact, at times she longed for the day when she and Orra would be married, and they could be together and alone at last, without all her brothers and sisters constantly around.

Julia had been sixteen when Orra Crosby entered her life. At twenty-one, he was much older than she, and strikingly handsome. And he had impressed Julia's family with his sincerity and determination. After all, he had walked all the way to Stevens' Mills, Vermont, from

The Lamoille River with the site of one of Samuel Stevens' mills.

Croydon, New Hampshire, with no more than hope of securing a job at Julia's father's mills. Julia remembered the day Orra had arrived there, all his belongings on his back

and "not a dollar to his name."[1] Orra had asked Julia's father, Samuel Stevens, for a job in either his sawmill or gristmill, explaining that he had already served his apprenticeship in the cloth-dressing trade in Newport. Her father had taken him on, and Orra had quickly proven himself to be hard-working and trustworthy. Over the years, Samuel and Puah Stevens had become quite fond of Orra—but not as fond as Julia had become. In time, Julia had gotten to know Orra well, first as her father's employee, then as a family friend. Gradually, however, their feelings for one another had become unavoidably obvious, and they began to spend more and more time together.

Julia had been naïve and carefree in those days, and so in love. She had felt warm and protected in Orra's loving embraces, secure in his maturity. But, almost exactly on her twentieth birthday, womanhood and motherhood overtook Julia.

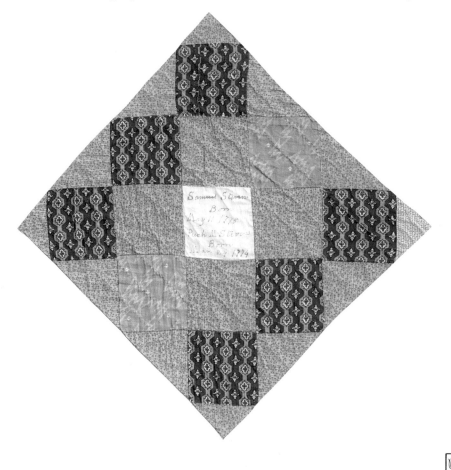

Samuel Stevens' brick house, East Hardwick (Stevens' Mills), Vermont.
Samuel and Puah's plank house stood nearby; their early log cabin,
where Julia was born, sat across the road.

She and Orra were married by the Justice of the Peace in Hardwick,[2] two miles from Stevens' Mills, on April 28, 1818. Five months later, Julia went into labor and gave birth to a healthy baby boy, Calvin Stevens Crosby.

After months, even years, of hoping, dreaming, planning for her wedding and married life, it had all happened so quickly, so unexpectedly. As if overnight, Julia was married and with a child of her own. And Orra, his responsibilities and ambitions now those of a family man, moved his young wife and son up the hill from the mills into a house beside his own cloth-dressing and wool-carding building, the only such business nearby. Julia tried to help her husband as well as care for the baby, cook, bake, wash, sew, spin, knit; her tasks were endless. Still, Julia knew she was not alone. She had her brothers and sisters and parents, Puah and Samuel, within short walking distance. She could even see smoke curling from the chimney of their plank house on the other side of the small village. Julia wondered how her mother had managed: Puah had given birth to her first child, Julia, inside a humble, drafty log cabin in the fiercest part of winter, amidst below-zero temperatures and dangerous snowstorms. Her family's very survival had depended on the red coals in the hearth and the ingenuity of herself and her husband. Samuel and Puah and their newborn, Julia, were isolated in this mountain wilderness along the Lamoille River in northern Vermont. Their nearest neighbors were two miles away, through a treacherous expanse of dense forest, in the newly settled small village of Hardwick.

In those early winters, Puah had no one to turn to for help. There was no one out there in the wilderness, as Julia now had, to teach her to make tallow candles for light or to save ashes and fat for soap, to help her make clothing for her baby, quilts to keep warm, brown bread and bean porridge for sustenance. No, Puah had to bring these skills with her. Except for her husband and infant, she was alone.

In time, though, Samuel Stevens' mills near their cabin on the river had thrived, and he had been better able to provide for Puah, Julia and the new little ones with even some special store-bought goods from the general stores in Hardwick and Greensboro. And, when Julia was about five, Samuel had moved his young family across the road into the newly completed plank house he had built from clapboards sawed at his own sawmill.

*L*ike their parents, Julia and Orra had nurtured a family and a business. The years sped by. In 1825, Julia had four young children: Calvin, Polly, Puah and their new baby John Quincey [sic] Adams, named after the new President.

Julia felt pride in the men in her life: her husband had become very respected in Stevens' Mills — in fact, in much of Caledonia County. Over the years he was selected to serve as a representative, justice and judge of the county, as well as the director of the Danville bank. Julia's father was also highly respected, and influential in his fight for temperance in his mills and in the village. His mill business was a growing success: he was known over the countryside for honesty and integrity in all his business dealings. From Julia's house on the hill in the village, she could now see brick chimneys across the river on the next crest; her father had completed a three-story brick house recently, and it crowned the hill and the village named after him.

With easier times in Stevens' Mills had come two more children for Julia: Seraphine, born January

22, 1833, and Flora, June 9, 1835. Unlike in the earlier years of their marriage, Julia and Orra could now give these girls nice things: a well-provided, comfortable home; pretty imported calicoes and silks for their dresses; even a good horse to ride. They would be taught in the Stevens tradition to be ladies, their schooling consisting only of learning to "read, write and cipher plausibly." More importantly, they would master the tasks women had to perform, such as "sewing a very fine seam, one that could not be seen,"[3] knitting and making beautiful quilts.

The next few years were terribly sad ones for Julia, beginning with her father's death in 1838. She would deeply miss her father, and she regretted that her daughters Seraphine and Flora would never really know their fine grandfather; they were too young, at five and three. And the brick house and village were different now without her father, even though her mother lived there with Julia's brother Joseph and younger sisters Ursula and Sarah.

But there was to be more sadness for Julia and her family. In 1842, her brother Simeon, the only Stevens to have graduated from the University of Vermont, without warning died quickly of "sore throat"[4] (pertussis), leaving a wife and child. In December of that same year, Julia lost her eldest daughter Polly, who was only twenty-two. Polly's body was buried in the cemetery on the road above the Stevens' brick house near that of her grandfather Samuel Stevens. With all this grief, Julia and her sisters had been worried about their mother's failing health. Three years later, Puah died, leaving her son Joseph heir to the brick house and mills as well as to the vast amount of land her husband had acquired.

*J*ulia thought back on how quickly the years had passed. It was 1860: all her children were married and having children of their own. Her eldest, Calvin, had married Lucy Brock from Newbury, Vermont in September 1843 and

was a farmer nearby. Her daughter Puah had married into the wealthy French family in the village, her son John to his neighbor Julia Sawyer. Even her baby girls were recently married, each of them to doctors—Flora to Andrew Hyde and Seraphine to Sherburne Leonard Wiswell. Flora and Andrew were living with Julia and Orra, a baby due soon; Seraphine was living in Hyde Park, Vermont, but would soon settle in Cabot, where her husband would establish an extensive practice.[5]

And the village of Stevens' Mills had also changed drastically. Julia remembered her childhood there, the early settlers, their cabins, the primitive roads through the forest. She had heard the men remark how in those years they had found their way through the "dense forest, by blazed trees," that they "could see but a few rods into the great woods."[6] But now Julia could look over her father's vast lands and beyond and see large farms, fine residences, flourishing businesses and the Congregational Church her

Early view of East Hardwick, Vermont, with Samuel Stevens' brick house in the far right background, from near the site of Julia and Orra Crosby's home. Photograph courtesy of Blanche Earle.

family had attended since she was a little girl. Sadly for Julia, with her father's and mother's passing, the name of Stevens' Mills had also been changed. The village was now called East Hardwick and, along with that change, much of the early history had been forgotten. The graveyard on the hill was slowly

gathering all that story into its bosom.

Julia walked down the hill and across the covered bridge, the Stevens sawmill on one side, the gristmill on the other. She continued walking, past her father's brick house. At the fork in the road, she turned right onto the narrow dirt road lined with straight, enormous pine trees that had stood there long before her father had come. She reached Sanborn Cemetery and placed flowers on her daughter's, mother's and father's graves. From where she stood, Julia looked out over the gorgeous valley, the azure Green Mountains in the distance.

Much of this land had once belonged to her father; he had been its first settler.

Indeed, Julia had a proud heritage, one that went back a century and a half in America. And her more recent ancestors had been among the first to brave the new Vermont frontier. Her grandfather Simeon Stevens and four of his brothers had served in the French and Indian War under Captain Jacob Bayley, and it was due to Bayley's foresight, advice and influence that, in 1762, Grandfather Simeon at twenty-six years of age had headed for a brand-new settlement called Newbury, Vermont. By canoe, with an old hunter to guide them, he and three others had glided down the winding Pemigewasset and Baker Rivers through the pine-laden White Mountains. It had taken Simeon and his entourage four days to reach their destination, the western banks of the Connecticut River. Then, on a meadow

overlooking the river, with a view of the White Mountains of his home state on the other side, Simeon had cleared the virgin forest and erected one of the first log houses in that part of Vermont. That same year he had married Sarah Hadley, who over the years bore him eleven children. Simeon, like Julia's maternal grandfather John Mellen, had been a captain in the Revolutionary War, his wife Sarah having died while he was away for the "Defense of the Frontier." Then, several years later, in 1788, Simeon had died also.

Julia's father, Samuel, had been only thirteen when his father Simeon died. He was soon apprenticed to a millwright. As soon as his apprenticeship was completed, Samuel had set out northwest from Newbury on the Bayley-Hazen Road (the military road opening the north-central part of Vermont and built by his father's friends Jacob Bayley and Moses Hazen) and headed for Greensboro, Vermont, where his brother Levi owned the mill. Samuel wanted his own land on a river, so he could also have a mill; in 1796, he walked down the narrow but straight Bayley-Hazen Road until he came to the remote, new little clearing of Hardwick, where men were busy felling and splitting timber and erecting log houses. Looking for a site for his mill, Samuel left the "Street" and forged his way through the dense, dark forest along the bank of the rock-bedded, shimmering Lamoille "until he came to the falls in the river where the village of East Hardwick now stands." It was then that he had stuck his willow whip into the ground, saying, "Here is where I am going to set my stakes."[7]

Within the year, Samuel had returned to Greensboro and married Puah Mellen. Puah was from Fitz-william, New Hampshire, and had

Julia Stevens Crosby.
Photograph courtesy of
Jane C. McKay.

been staying with her married sister in Greensboro when she had first met her future husband. Samuel soon brought his new bride through miles of towering pine and spruce to his sunlit little clearing. There sat a small cabin with a rough stone chimney: Puah's new home. The continuously rushing Lamoille and calls of their wild animal neighbors echoed around them. Samuel had unlatched the log door to the cabin and helped Puah inside. It was dark inside the small cabin, with mixed smells of wood, mustiness and dampness. Leaving the door open for light, they had eaten their first meal "over a chest which contained about all their earthly possessions."[8] During their first

winter there, little Julia had been born.

Now it was sixty-four years since her father had first picked out this forested river valley for Puah's and his home. How could Julia preserve something of her parents and earlier ancestors? She did want her children to remember.

Her answer, her only means of creativity and lasting expression, was in needlework. Julia began making blocks for a friendship quilt, a very popular quilt at this time all over Vermont. She would make hers basically like others she had seen, using a simple block pattern repeated over the entire top and signing each block in ink. Julia would include her ancestors no

longer living, along with her present family. That was not such an uncommon idea. But Julia would take the idea of a friendship quilt one step further, making hers quite unusual: she would write the date of birth under each person's name on her quilt. In that way, the blocks on her quilt would record life. Julia made at least two such quilts: one for her eldest son, Calvin, and his wife, Lucy Brock; the other for Seraphine and her husband, Sherburne Wiswell. Except for the number of blocks included and overall size, Julia made the quilts identical, with the same cherry-wreath quilting pattern, signatures and cotton prints. There was only one exception to this: she added the Brocks (Robert, Sabra S. and John) to Calvin's quilt, for his wife's family, and Lucy and Leonard Wiswell to Seraphine's to include her in-laws. Julia's friendship quilts were simple ones, neatly and carefully made, yet in their simplicity they served their purpose as important records for her children.

Shortly after Julia finished these quilts, her youngest granddaughter, Julia R. Hyde (Flora's child), died. Little Julia had been the most recent birth in the family at the time Julia was making her quilts; now this child was the first death in the family after the quilts' completion. The family was devastated. Flora and her husband, grief-stricken, selected an unusual, delicately ornamented, small monument of love for their little girl. The other record of this little one was on Julia's quilts. Her quilts went hand in hand with the stones in the cemetery, her quilt blocks showing life, the gravestones death. Julia could have added those dates of deaths to her quilts, but she did not; the stones in the cemetery were permanent enough.

Two and one-half years after their granddaughter's death, Julia's and Orra's eldest son, Calvin, died.

With his death, Julia and Orra decided to accept their daughter Seraphine's offer to move into her large Victorian mansion in Cabot, Vermont, eight miles away. Orra, at seventy-three, was not well and no longer able to do much of the work himself, and Seraphine and Dr. Wiswell had live-in help and nineteen rooms. Sherburne and Seraphine provided a comfortable life for her elderly parents in their ornate three-story house, but Orra died only a few years later, of consumption, in 1872.

Orra had amassed a large fortune with his cloth-dressing and wool-carding business, his success as a politician and, most recently, his presidency of the Caledonia National Bank at Danville, Vermont; therefore, after his death, Seraphine received a substantial inheritance.

Gravestone of Julia R. Hyde.

In addition to the money, however, Seraphine had also inherited her father's astute business sense, and quickly invested in Western mortgages, soon tripling her inheritance

by foreclosing on properties when the mortgages came due, destroying optimistic young men very much like her own grandfather had been when he had founded Stevens' Mills in 1796.

*J*ulia lay in bed in an upstairs room in her daughter's immense house. Her once-shining, long brown hair was now a cap of dull gray upon her head. Her once-radiant, beautiful face was now masked over by time and hard work, and her brown eyes, once sparkling, vibrant and expressive, were now weary. From the floor below, she could hear the muffled voices of her daughter Seraphine and son-in-law Sherburne. They were having another spat, probably over money. Seraphine was always so frugal,

The Wiswell mansion, Cabot, Vermont.

even though she had a great deal of money. She knitted face cloths from packaging string and shorted the neighbor boy a penny or two for the packets of pine he delivered. Her husband, Sherburne, was so different: he was such a kind man and never cared if his patients were able to pay, and it always angered Seraphine so when he accepted produce as payment.

While Seraphine was fighting for temperance, Dr. Wiswell was working for birth control, telling "the farmers they were abusing their wives having so many children." And Julia remembered Dr. Wiswell's work during the Civil War. For those men who requested it, he pulled their teeth, since the army would not take anyone who could not chew hardtack.[9]

Julia's life had been so different from her daughter Seraphine's, although they were only one generation apart. Julia had known hard times, lean times. She had known

Seraphine Crosby Wiswell. Photograph courtesy of Jane C. McKay.

extremes, such as the time in 1816, just before she was married, when snow had fallen in June and devastated all the crops for miles around. Food was so scarce that year that

"boys and girls would eat birch twigs and beech leaves, and anything they could get to eat, and they called it good."[10] And, during most of her youth, Julia had worn unfashionable homespun, even coarse tow and scratchy worsteds. Imported figured calicoes and muslins, the fashion then, were expensive and scarce, especially where Julia lived. Seraphine would never understand such hardships or value her fine things as Julia had. For years and years, Julia had always had to work so hard, making everything her family needed in order to live; Seraphine did not: she had a girl to do everything in her house, even to make tea.

There were wood stoves now in place of hearths, oil lamps instead of candles, cakes of soap for sale at the store, even sewing machines. Julia's daughter had time now for fashionable pastimes like painting floral pictures and playing her pianoforte. And travel was different now too. Julia's grandfather Simeon had come to Vermont by canoe, her father had ventured farther north by foot, but now the train had reached this part of Vermont and was completely changing the development of towns like Stevens' Mills.

Life quietly and gently slipped away from Julia that eighty-first year of her life. The large Crosby monument near Julia's mother and father, in the cemetery of East Hardwick, was engraved under her husband's name and death,

Julia His Wife
Died July 30, 1879
A.E. 81 Years.

Although Julia was gone, the Stevens family was still prominent in East Hardwick; her brother Joseph, his wife, daughter and adopted child Kate were now living in the Samuel Stevens brick house. A stern, big-boned man with thick sideburns, Joseph was following in his father's footsteps, being adamantly against any alcoholic drink and, along with his family, a pious member of the Congregational Church there. But within ten years, due to tragedy and death, Joseph's family and the Stevens estate were no more. Joseph's rifle accidentally discharged as he stepped out of his carriage, killing him, and his wife and daughter died suddenly of influenza, leaving eighteen-year-old Kate as sole heir in 1889. But Kate, only recently having been told she was adopted, had a great deal of pain, bitterness and disillusionment as to her identity. She quickly sold all the Stevens property, including the brick house, and left to be with her "real family" in Amesbury, Massachusetts. All of Samuel and Puah Stevens' possessions were scattered about, Kate taking some and selling the rest.

Strangely enough, Seraphine Wiswell, Julia's daughter, would be the one to preserve what was left of the Stevens' heritage. Seraphine's house was large, and she kept all of her mother's belongings exactly as they had been when her mother had lived there. And her family after her have continued to keep the Victorian mansion in Cabot as Seraphine left it, with Julia's imported French silk gown and her children's mid-century red and rose-sprigged calico dresses still hanging in the large walk-in closet in the rear second-floor bedroom. Julia's and Orra's pictures are still hanging on the living-room wall; her flax wheel is under the stairwell in the entryway.

In Seraphine's upstairs closet, only one of Julia's quilts remains, the one she made for her son Calvin. It probably had been returned to Julia after his early death in 1866. The other quilt was sold, and is the one in this book. They were such plain, simple quilts, so nearly identical in every detail, that the decision had been made to keep only one of them. But on them Julia had given life — immortality — to herself and her family. For on those quilts, one would see *only* the joyous celebration of their births, and that was the way Julia had intended, so many years earlier when she had made her friendship quilts.

But how many identical quilts were there in all? Had she not intended to be fair and to make one of these quilts for each of her children? Were there not, then, possibly five quilts? If that is so, there are still three missing quilts (Puah French's, Flora Hyde's and John Q. A. Crosby's) somewhere with more of the pieces of the living record of Julia's family's heritage inked on them.

Julia Stevens Crosby's silk dress, c. 1840, found in the Wiswell mansion, Cabot, Vermont.

June
1892.

Cousin.
Lida Kepley
Golden.
Kan.

Willie

Mar.
1893.
Cousin.
Stella Kepley.
Golden.
Kan.

Cousin
Viola

Fannie.

Fannie's Missing Quilt

*I*n
the early seventies, I found my first
friendship quilt hanging on a rack at the
Rose Bowl Flea Market in Pasadena, California.
In perfect condition, the quilt was composed of thirty
blocks of the *Chimney Sweep* pattern, each embroidered
in red cotton floss with a person's name, his or her relationship to the quiltmaker, a town and state, a month and
a year (ranging from 1891 to 1894). The quiltmaker
had not included her name on the quilt, but from the
relationships indicated, I determined that her
maiden name was Cord, her married name
Harris, and I hoped to find out
her first name soon.

She was from Golden, Kansas, but where *was* Golden? The town did not seem to exist. For several years, I searched for it; finally the Kansas State Historical Society Library at Topeka located Golden in a dead-town file. It was a town in existence for only nine years. The early settlers had planted their first wheat there in 1887, but by 1894 (the date when the last of the quilt blocks were completed), most of them had moved away. In 1900, there were only 422 people remaining in all of Grant County.

However, I soon discovered that the people whose names were on my quilt had been the ones to endure the scorching summer heat, the strong, hot winds, the disastrous droughts and grasshopper plagues; many of those early pioneers' descendants were still in the area, having settled in nearby Ulysses after Golden failed. I began talking to those Kansans by telephone and soon was in touch with the descendants of the quiltmaker, whose name I found to be Frances Malinda Cord Harris, known to all of her family as "Fannie."

In August of 1981, I took Fannie's quilt back to Ulysses, to the Pioneer Settlers' Picnic. In that room of 250 people were many of the descendants of those first pioneers of Golden, Kansas. Fannie's quilt embodied the pioneer spirit of Golden that these people had gathered to celebrate. Indeed, this was *their* quilt.

It was one of the most moving, most memorable experiences of my life when the elderly and the young alike, with glistening, teary eyes and smiles of wonderment on their faces, gazed upon the embroidered names of their grandmothers, great-aunts, even great-great-grandmothers. One white-haired, crippled, feeble little lady, nearly one hundred years old, who had appeared unable to see or hear the afternoon's program, was carefully and ever so slowly helped to a chair at the table's edge where I had spread Fannie's quilt out for all to see. As she jerkily began moving her crooked fingers over names, joy lighted up her face, as if she were seeing her friends again right there in that quilt.

I began a friendship with Fannie's family that weekend and spent many hours talking with them about their grandmother and her life. Our conversations and correspondence have continued since then. I have talked with eight of Fannie's grandchildren: John Ralph McGillivray, Mary Frances McGillivray Hickok, Nola McGillivray Hampton, Jim McGillivray, Billie Lou Harris Smiley, Dorothy Smiley, Eve Campbell and Glenna Wiruth. They are the children of Fannie's daughters Hattie and Bessie and son Charlie. I have also spent time with Fannie's great-granddaughter Barbara McGillivray Lewis, daughter of Hattie's son George. Their mixed recollections tell Fannie's story.

*F*annie was "born in Indiana in around Russelville in 1858, December 29. I think she was Irish

Simeon Cord, Fannie's father.
Photograph courtesy of
Mary Frances McGillivray Hickok,
Fannie's granddaughter.

maby a little dutch."[1] Her father, Simeon Cord, and his parents were all born in Kentucky; her mother, Margaret Caroline Eckard, was born and lived her short life in Indiana. "When Fannie was four years old, her mother fainted and fell into an open fireplace. Fannie ran to get help (she was the oldest of the girls), but her mother died from being burnt so bad. Fannie's father married again. In all, he was married three times, so Fannie had four sisters and eight half brothers and half sisters. His last wife, Nan, was a lot younger than himself."

On October 21, 1877, at eighteen years of age, Fannie married George Harvey Harris. Four children, Hattie, Charlie, Manford and Myrtie, were born to them in Russellville, Indiana. Then Fannie and George moved to Golden. "The trend was to go west. Old Grandpa Kepley's family [Fannie's relatives] came here first in 1887. Then the Harrises came to Grant County, in October of that year. They just put all their things in a boxcar. They came out here on the train from Putnam County [Indiana] to Hartland, seven miles west of Lakin. Then they made a cut south through the sand hills. The Kepleys even had an ox team. I think Grandpa [George Harvey Harris] must have had a milk cow.

"Grandma and Grandpa had never seen this kind of country. You could pick up buffalo horns on the prairie; all of the land was covered with buffalo grass. Once they got here, they had no choice but to stay: they didn't have enough money to go back to Indiana. Grandma's family [the Kepleys] came from about the same place. And Grandpa Harris had some livestock, so he had to have some land. This was all new here. There were no graded roads, only sand, but you could go anywhere on a horse — just all grass.

"They'd go out to Lakin thirty miles after a load of coal. People would get the staples there. They hauled groceries, coal and everything by team and wagon. I'm pretty sure Momma [Fannie's daughter Hattie] said there was a little grocery store at Golden. There was a post office and a blacksmith shop

School, Golden, Kansas, c. 1894. Photograph courtesy of Ray Kepley.

in Golden, too. Two or three families lived there. The schoolhouse was about a mile south of the cemetery and a little west.

"When Grandpa went to breaking the sod, he only had a horse and a cow. The cow had a steer calf. He worked them. Put the harness on the steer. Grandpa Harris didn't even have a yoke."

The men in Kansas were ranchers. "They farmed just enough to feed their cattle in the winter. Those cattle were wild — and I mean *wild*. Big-horn steers. You'd hear those horns a-hitting each other."

Bessie Pearl was Fannie and George's first child conceived and born in Kansas, a little more than a year later. Their sixth child, Clara Olive, was born two years later on

March 4, 1891, but she lived only ten days and was buried in the little Golden Cemetery in the middle of the vast prairie.

"At that time they'd just drive a stake up with a name. Over the years that would rot. There were two little graves so close together, and we never knew for sure which one Clara was buried in. We always put flowers on both of those graves, and that way we think we got hers. She was just a baby."

It was only two months after little Clara's funeral that Fannie received the first signed block for her friendship quilt. Her sister-in-law Mollie Harris sent it from Gower, Missouri, that May of 1891. Of her five living children, Fannie included only her three daughters, Hattie, Myrtie and little three-year-old Bessie, the baby of the family. She did not add her sons', or even her husband's, names to her quilt. For the most part, each woman or girl stitched her own block out of a piece of her own cloth for Fannie's quilt; no two blocks are of the same cotton. Fannie's sister Eva Carrington, who was married and still living in Russellville, however, made a special, creative block for her sister: instead of using only one printed cotton, she reached into her scrap bag and chose twelve different little prints.

It took Fannie over three years to collect all of her blocks. With the one for her baby half sister Pearl Cord from Mayview, Illinois, dated June 1894, finally finished, Fannie alternated the thirty signed blocks with plain white ones, sewing them all together with her machine. That, she believed, was best for stitching long seams, but not for quilting. After basting the top, cotton batt and bleached white muslin backing together, Fannie propped her quilting frames onto the backs of chairs. Then she carefully began quilting the delicate feathers she had earlier traced from her template. Her quilting stitches were tiny and straight, for she was a perfectionist in almost everything she did. She wanted her friendship quilt to be a special quilt, so she could always be proud of it.

*H*attie was married, with a baby of her own, and Bessie was only nine, when Fannie and George moved their family to Edmond, Norton County, Kansas "in the spring of '98." Only Hattie, her husband and young family remained behind. "They [Fannie and George] had lived in Indiana, where there were more trees. I think the Harmons [cousins] went up there first to Norton. Grandma and Grandpa thought that would be a lot nicer, and Charlie, their older boy, was up there in Nebraska.

"Up there, Grandpa made a rock house. He got rocks out of the canyon and split them up. Plowed the dirt off of it with oxen and used dynamite to get it out. Then he used a team of horses to pull the rocks up. The walls were

about eighteen inches thick: they were really put in there good. The rock walls are still there, but the windows and doors are gone. A bunch of cattle were there in the house a few years ago.

"I think Grandma and Grandpa lived in a dugout while Grandpa was building the rock house. I remember there was a dugout right close to the house. It was dug down into the ground deep. They used to keep ice there in the wintertime.

Kepley family portrait. Back row, left to right: Edward, Anna, Lida, Belle and Frank. Middle row, left to right: Grandpa (David) Kepley, Emma, Stella, Grandma Manda. Front row, left to right: Viola, Dolpha, Clarence and Elodie. Photograph courtesy of Nellie Burr Lattimore.

"My dad [Hattie's husband, Ed] was in the legislature then in Topeka. When my sister Helen was six weeks old, he took us up to Edmond in the covered wagon pulled with four horses. It took five or six days to get there. We had to ford the rivers—might be a foot deep of water and there'd be ice on the streams. He left us children with Grandma. Us kids slept in the covered wagon part of the time while Grandpa was building the stone house. It was a big regular wagon with a canvas top that was wider than the wagon box. We had

some beds in there. We'd have what we wanted to eat and enough quilts to keep warm."

It was about this time that Fannie discovered that her daughter Bessie had diabetes, the reason that she had been sick so much of her young life. "I remember when we'd go up there in the covered wagon to stay, Grandma'd have things we weren't allowed to have, like great big oranges. We kids thought they looked so good. In those days we

didn't have many oranges: there wasn't any train down where we lived, and where they lived, they had a railroad about three or four miles away, and they could get oranges. Of course, they were real expensive. We'd ask Grandma why Bessie could have an orange, and we couldn't, and she'd say, 'You can have candy; Bessie can't.'"

At first, Fannie, George and the children had to live in a dugout, then in the cellar of the house while George finished the ground floor. But Fannie did not complain. She was used to much harder times than these down in Golden. She worked hard: "She could just work all day. She never had time even to go to church while George was alive. He wanted her to go with him, but Fannie always thought the farm had to have attention. She stayed home and worked so her husband could go." Fannie also stayed home on Sundays to make the meal, because the minister was coming for dinner—fried chicken and homemade pie. After George died, she "never missed church." She still had all the work to do, "she just went anyway."

Fannie followed a rigid work schedule. She washed on Mondays. "Her washing machine was out on the porch. It was one of those tumble kind. You'd push and pull the handle. We kids used to think it was fun to go to her home on washday on that account."

Every Tuesday, she ironed. "I can remember her ironing in the summer—they wore a lot of petticoats then—she would heat the iron on the stove. It was so hot, I asked her if she had to do that. She cooked on a range stove, and Grandpa had fixed her a sink and a cistern outside." Later Fannie had a cistern with a pump in her kitchen.

Along with her household tasks, Fannie tended her peach orchard of fifteen to twenty trees—"white peaches . . . they were so good." And she took care of her garden. She raised Plymouth Rock chickens and "lots of turkeys," as well as cared for the pigs, cows and horses.

Somehow Fannie found time to do "a lot of quilting. Her quilts were mostly calico prints. Some of the patterns of the lighter ones were good. In the darker ones, she just

kind of put pieces together. I don't know where the material came from. They did have a general store at Edmond, though. The quilting frames were plain at that time, and Fannie always put hers on the backs of chairs."

As the years passed, except for Manford, all of Fannie's children married and moved into their own homes. And Fannie soon had many grandchildren. In spite of the overabundance of work, she was never too busy to have them visit or stay with her. And sometimes they would surprise her with a visit, and she'd say, "I just told Manford this morning, my nose has just been itching all day. I *told* him we were going to have company."

Fannie's grandchildren remember her one-story house with the old range and heating stove in the kitchen. "As you went into the front

Harris family portrait. Standing, left to right: Myrtie, Charlie, Hattie, Manford and Bessie. Seated: George and Fannie.
Photograph courtesy of Mary Frances McGillivray Hickok.

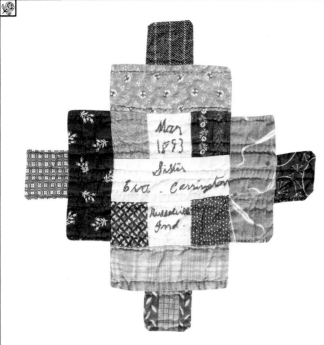

door, you faced the old wood-burning range. Above that was a partially closed cupboard where you could see some of Fannie's pots and pans. To the left of the front door, there was a big — at least three feet deep — bay window filled with geraniums and other flowers that bloomed all winter. There were shades on the windows, no curtains then. It was always so bright in there." Over the kitchen table hung a Coleman lamp. "One day I said, 'Oh, Grandma, I'd like to have that

lamp someday.' 'George,' she said, 'get up there and take that lamp down.' Grandma gave things like that. She was very generous." To the right of the kitchen was the first bedroom, Fannie and George's bedroom. When one of the grandchildren stayed overnight, the child would sleep in the middle of the big feather bed, with Fannie and George on either side. "Fannie's feather beds had more feathers in them than anyone else's. The thing would come up and practically

smother you." In between the two bedrooms and connecting with her kitchen was "quite a long pantry, like a small kitchen working area. Fannie made her cakes in there because everything was handy." She also stored all her canned fruit and vegetables on shelves there. "She raised and always canned everything."

Behind the kitchen and "facing the roadway and wood porch" was Fannie's parlor. "She kept that closed off. Children never dared

Chimney Sweep, by Frances Malinda Cord Harris, Golden, Kansas, 1891–1894, 77 ½ × 65 ½ inches, pieced cottons.

go in there unless there was company." There was "a green, brown and floral-colored Axminster rug about nine by twelve with quite a pretty pattern, then the varnished floor around that." On one wall was "an old organ (I never saw her play it)." Her settee, "more like a day bed," was always covered with a quilt. There were a couple of big, sturdy rocking chairs, other simple furnishings and kerosene lamps.

Of course, "there was no indoor plumbing. The privy was about one hundred feet from the house. It had three holes. There was always a 'Sears and Roebuck' hanging on a string for paper."

For years and years, Fannie's children and grandchildren would come to her house for big Thanksgiving and Christmas dinners. "We'd eat in the cellar at first. I remember once she cooked a little pig with an apple in its mouth and she served it head and all. As she was walking around the table and putting all the food on, she'd keep glancing at it. Then she said, 'You know, whenever I see that little pig with the apple in its mouth, I always get the shitters'—she meant to say 'shivers.' We all laughed so hard, and she was always so embarrassed."

At Fannie's house, the grownups ate first. Fannie wanted everything to look good to them. "The children would be in the other room screaming and hollering while the grownups would sit at the table for two to three hours just eating and talking."

"Fannie was a little bit of a woman. She was a little, fast, quick Irish woman. She never walked in her life—she always ran. She'd just fly with her feet. She had brown-

119

black eyes, was about four feet seven inches with black, heavy hair. It wasn't real curly. Her husband and she were quite a contrast. George was six feet two. When George held his arm out, Fannie could stand under it. George was a very fine, gentle, religious man. He was the nearest perfect man I ever knew. He never did anything except for somebody else, and he just worshipped Fannie. She couldn't have a fuss with him if she wanted to—he'd do what he wanted to anyway."

But Fannie, healthy, energetic and sprightly, was in the prime of her life when George "died real suddenly of a heart attack in the winter of 1920." And seven years later, when Fannie was sixty-eight and living in the rock house in Edmond with her son Manford, she received word that her eldest daughter in Ulysses, Hattie, widowed with four children aged eight to eighteen still at home, had died suddenly of a stroke at forty-eight years of age.

This was a time of great sadness in Fannie's life; yet, she bounced back. It was as if she had already lived one life. Her trip to her daughter's funeral in Ulysses and the Golden area brought a close to the first one, and Fannie returned to Norton County to begin a second life with many industrious, good years ahead.

*I*n her later years, Fannie's grandchildren began to wonder at her strange behavior. For example, whenever it would storm, Fannie would run outside with cups and other containers in order to save all the rainwater she could. These children were unaware of the years of drought in Golden—years of suffering and hardship, when each drop of water had been precious. Fannie now had a windmill within

thirty feet of her house, and "within that was running well water." The water went into a refrigeration basin in which Fannie kept her food cold. There were little troughs so the water ran off into her garden. "Grandma had all the water she needed; she didn't need to save any more."

Fannie in old age. Photograph courtesy of Barbara McGillivray Lewis, Fannie's great-granddaughter.

And there were other strange things she did. One time her granddaughter took her home and noticed Fannie's shoes were on the wrong feet. When she pointed that out, Fannie explained, "The heels have worn off the other way, so I wanted to balance them up."

Fannie's only mirror "always looked contorted." When she was about ninety, Bessie's children wondered how Grandma "could tell anything in it," but Fannie explained that she was used to it. Later, however, Fannie looked into a mirror at her daughter's house and said, "Well, Bessie, I look like an old woman." Privately, Bessie's daughter remarked to her mother, "I

understand why she would think she looked old if she got a good mirror."

All her life, even in Golden, Fannie had dressed in conservative "long calico or percale dresses, dark ones in the winter, lighter in the summer, and she always wore an apron over her dress." But when she was in her eighties and nineties, she'd have "long underwear on with one leg pulled up, the other one down. She'd look like the dickens. She'd always have a dirty apron on that might be black as the ace of spades; yet, she was absolutely spotless in her cooking. She was a perfectionist—a good cook. Her noodle soup was so good. Her secret: 'When I cook an old hen to make soup, I put a bay leaf in it.' She also made great fried chicken and pies and white cake with whipped cream and halves of walnuts on the top. I don't think any of us ever saw an imperfect walnut on it. She cracked them all herself." Besides her white cake, Fannie made a delicious chocolate cake with sour cream that was "real dark reddish brown."

And Fannie never stopped raising her chickens. "When she was in her nineties, she'd get up the ladder to get the eggs and baby chickens in the hayloft. Manford was so worried she'd fall that he took the ladder down. Then she just had an awful time to get the eggs. She took a rope and threw it over the rafters. She fixed her some boxes or improvised somehow and climbed up there and got the baby chicks. She was real strong. Manford just laughed and laughed when he got home. Here he thought he would keep her from falling by taking the ladder down, but she got up there anyway.

"Later Fannie did fall and break her hip. Then she had pneumonia. She died in the hospital in Norton at ninety-three."

Fannie's grandchildren and great-grandchildren all loved her, and they remember her as a strong pioneer woman and a wonderful grandmother. They remember with a smile, even laughter, her quickness, her spirit and her funny ways. Many of the things she said and did were strange, like her fretting over one of her quilts. It had worried her so. She kept saying that someone had stolen it. Her grandchildren thought she was senile. They always tried to calm her by assuring her she had all her quilts. But it was to no avail; Fannie continued to worry.

Her grandchildren could not understand what Fannie was talking about: "The woman had a whole lot of quilts. There was a trunk of quilts. She had quilts on all the beds. She'd have us air the quilts because she was afraid the moths would get them. They were something that she loved. I don't know who made them, but they meant something to her." Down in Golden, "they made all their quilts. They made quilts all the time. I can remember them having quilting bees. The Kepleys were the ones to have enough money. They'd have dinner and all get together."

Fannie missed her special quilt, but no one knew which quilt that was. She had so many, her grandchildren thought possibly she had given one away and then forgotten. It was not until my trip to Ulysses in 1981 that the mystery of Fannie's missing quilt was solved. When I showed Fannie's friendship quilt to her eldest granddaughter and namesake, Mary Frances, she remembered, "I have seen this quilt at Grandma's house several times. She put it on the porch just like her good bedspread, but she didn't let anybody sleep on it. She treasured it. It was her best quilt.

"It comes back to me very plain. She kept it in a box. It had a card or piece of paper on it with her name and 'Golden, Kansas.' She had it in an old-fashioned trunk behind the door in her bedroom. That was about the last time I saw it. I am sure she made it. She had to have made it. No one else would have. That was kind of a fad. 'If you'd make me a block, I'd make you a block.'" And Mary's youngest sister Nola added, "Everybody made a friendship quilt. You had no TV; you just sat and pieced a quilt. You couldn't buy a blanket: there wasn't a blanket to buy."

In late 1981, I received a letter from Mary Frances: "My granddaughters were so interested in the quilt, that they want me to help them make a copy of yours." For the next year or so, I tried to help Mary by correspondence and telephone with the details of Fannie's quilt. It took Mary Frances McGillivray Hickok nearly two years to finish piecing all of her friendship quilt blocks. "All the people wrote the names on a piece of paper, and I carboned these onto the blocks." Then Mary embroidered over them. "I believe I finished the quilt in '83 before Christmas. I sent it to her [the quilter] in October of '83, and she sent it back at Christmas time." In 1984, Mary's friendship quilt won a blue ribbon at the Grant County Fair.

So now there are two friendship quilts spanning six generations of the Harris family and nearly one hundred years of Kansas history. It is appropriate that these people should immortalize their existence, for they have a deep-seated, rich devotion to *their* Kansas. Fannie's great-granddaughter Barbara summed up her family's love for their land when she told me, "I always thought I'd move back to Ulysses, but since my daddy's gone, I probably never will. I really miss the Kansas sunset. The Kansas sun feels so good...."

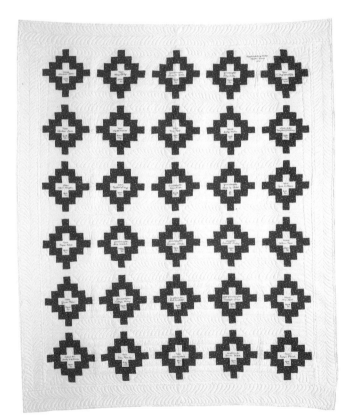

Chimney Sweep, by Mary Frances McGillivray Hickok, Ulysses, Kansas, 1983, 78 1/2 × 94 1/2 inches, pieced cottons and cotton blends. Quilted by Elsie Deakins. Collection of Mary Frances McGillivray Hickok.

Footnotes

I
Remember Me

1. Neal, "Chronological History," p. 39.

2. Neal, p. 40.

3. Patent No. 9701 by Juillier (1834) and patent No. 6118 by Dunand (1838). *Description des machines.*

4. U.S. Patent No. 2,176, 106-20.

5. Carvalho, *Forty Centuries*, p. 135.

6. *New York Morning Herald,* July 11, 1839, p. 4.

7. *New York Morning Herald,* p. 4.

8. Carvalho, p. 257.

9. *New York Morning Herald,* p. 4.

10. Finley, *The Lady of Godey's*, p. 177.

11. *Godey's Lady's Book,* X (March 1835), 136.

12. *The Lady's Book,* I (January 1831), 64. Although dated 1831, this magazine actually appeared in 1830.

13. *The Lady's Book,* IV (January 1832), 9.

14. *The Lady's Book,* IX (August 1834), 79.

15. *Godey's Lady's Book,* XVI (April 1838), 166.

16. *Godey's Lady's Book,* XVIII (April 1839), 153.

17. *Godey's Lady's Book,* XIX (July 1839), 19.

18. *Godey's Lady's Book,* XXII (April 1841), 146.

19. McMorris, *Crazy Quilts*, p. 11.

20. McMorris, p. 11.

21. *Godey's Lady's Book and Magazine,* CVII (November 1883), 493.

22. McMorris, p. 11.

23. Ellen E. Reed to Stedman and Arterista Spaulding (continuation of letter begun by J. W. Reed), March 17-19, 1856.

II
Betsey! I Wish You a Merry Christmas

1. Most of Betsey's daughters' names and initials are recorded in differing ways on documents, gravestones, pension papers and in Betsey's will. Sarah I. J. Lee was also called Belle; Betsey M. A. was nicknamed Bessie; Susan A. M. was known as Susie or Etta; Lelia N. L. was referred to as Lillie, Leilia or Nellie.

2. Randall and Donald, *The Civil War*, p. 314.

3. There is no written evidence that Abner sent money home to Betsey. However, as shown in the letter from Electa Blowers (see p. 55), responsible husbands sent their money home in order that their wives and children could survive. Abner had proven himself to be such a husband throughout his marriage to Betsey.

4. In existence for thirteen months, Andersonville Prison was an enclosure of about 16½ acres, later enlarged to 26½ acres. Within that small area, nearly 33,000 Union soldiers were held captive at the time Abner Lee was a prisoner. "In the one month of August nearly three thousand prisoners are reported to have died (approximately one hundred a day)." (Randall and Donald, p. 337.) Walt Whitman wrote of Confederate prisons, "All the horrors that can be named, starvation, lassitude, filth, vermin, despair, swift loss of self-respect, idiocy, insanity, and frequent murder, were there." (Whitman, "Specimen Days," *Complete Prose,* p. 48.)

5. Croffut and Morris, *The Military and Civil History,* p. 753.

6. Croffut and Morris, p. 752.

7. Croffut and Morris, p. 753.

8. Abner Lee's grave is now marked number 10,228 at Andersonville National Cemetery.
   Because of his penmanship, Dorence Atwater, a Connecticut prisoner at Andersonville, had the job of daily recording the names of the dead soldiers. Secretly, he kept a duplicate list. After leaving Andersonville (February 2, 1865), Atwater showed the list of 12,636 deceased prisoners to Clara Barton, who was working to locate missing and dead Union soldiers. She became convinced that with Atwater's list and government help she might be able to identify the graves at Andersonville "by comparing the numbered stakes marking each man's position in the burial trenches with the corresponding number listed by name in Atwater's register." Beginning in July of 1865, Clara Barton, along with Dorence Atwater and Captain James M. Moore and a crew of thirty-four men, began marking the graves of the Union soldiers. It is because of the diligence of Atwater and Barton that Abner Lee's grave is known today. (Strock, *Andersonville National Cemetery,* pp. 3-5.)

9. From the "Widow's Declaration for Pension" form that Betsey filled out on February 3, 1865. Note that Betsey did not know her husband's actual date of death. He had in fact died on October 2, 1864. (United States Government, National Archives, Washington, D.C.)

10. On all other military documents, and on his gravestone, Abner's death is given as October 2, 1864.

11. From the will of Sarah S. Wright, March 29, 1875, Putnam, Connecticut, Town Clerk's Office.

12. No record has been found as to what happened to Lillie. She was willed "one large silver spoon marked I. C. to J. M." in her grandmother's (Sarah S. Wright's) will of 1875, but Lillie's name does not appear in census records of Putnam, Connecticut, in 1880, and she is not listed in her mother's will, made December 30, 1887. Betsey wrote only "I give and bequeath to my two daughters Belle & Etta, share and share alike." (Putnam, Connecticut, Town Clerk's Office.)

13. In particular, there is one delicate, flowered fabric with a black-dotted brown background on the outside edge of the quilt. Because it was disintegrating, it was covered over by a new piece of fabric shortly after the quilt was completed. The author has since removed this newer fabric, returning the quilt to its original state.

14. These portraits were painted by the famous folk portraitist Winthrop Chandler, Betsey's great-great-uncle (brother of her great-grandfather Theophilus Chandler). For many years the portraits hung "in the house built [by Betsey's great-grandfather] and afterwards occupied by [Betsey's uncle] Charles Chandler, Esq., on Chandler Hill, Thompson, Conn., a part of the homestead farm of Capt. William Chandler [Betsey's great-great-grandfather]." (Chandler, *The Chandler Family*, p. 270.) These oil portraits now hang in the American Antiquarian Society, Worcester, Massachusetts.

15. From the diary of John May, made up of many small pieces of parchment folded to make a book. There is no cover. Begun in 1706, it chronicles two decades. Throughout his diary, John May utilizes symbology; for example, ☉ is used to denote the sun. On page 133 of the diary, Betsey practiced her capital B's for "Betsey," and on page 134, she practiced writing her name. (Collection of the American Antiquarian Society, Worcester, Massachusetts.)

16. (Compare footnote 13.) The author removed three pieces of fabric that had been carefully put over disintegrating original ones. She then covered the original fabric with netting to restore the quilt. In so doing, she opened the seam along one edge of the quilt, the width of one block, and discovered the message hidden there. The rest of the messages around the outside edges of the quilt are unknown because of her desire to keep the quilt in its original condition.

17. Betsey called it this when she made out her will. "Album" was a name popular at this time because of the renewed popularity of autograph album books.

18. From Betsey Wright Lee's will, in which she carefully listed all of her belongings, including the "embroidery that was [her] aunt Betsey Wrights," her "white knit spread," "one double Irish chain bed quilt," her "white spread worked in flowers with the letters worked on A.F.D," "one large spinning wheel," "nine linen sheets," as well as her "Poll Parrot and cage" and her "book called 'Wonders Of Prayer.'" (Putnam, Connecticut, Town Clerk's Office.)

III
Till Death Do Us Part

1. "Moses Blowers and Stutson Benson settled at an early day near Barber's on Lot 84." (*Re-union of . . . Pompey*, p. 207.) The Pompey-Delphi-Fabius area was a closely knit community. Pompey Four Corners was the early name of Delphi, which is now called Delphi Falls.

2. From years of family genealogical research gathered by a descendant of Moses Blowers, Norma Calkins Harger of Ann Arbor, Michigan, in a letter to the author dated October 1, 1984.

3. Many of the details of the Blowers family history are from the unpublished papers written by Roy K. Blowers of Danbury, Wisconsin. He has generously shared his years of hard work in numerous telephone conversations and letters.

4. Lucy's quilt blocks were all signed before her trip to Michigan in 1849: with one exception (a block signed "Lucy Lane Stanley, Wisconsin"), all the blocks on Lucy Blowers' quilt are from New York. There are none from Michigan. The births, marriages and deaths of persons whose names are inscribed place the quilt blocks at this time as well. The fabrics of the individual quilt blocks are typical of the 1840's, and the cottons used to back the quilt are also from this period.

5. From the unpublished papers of Roy K. Blowers.

6. The location of Henry and Lucy's wedding is found in Minister of the Gospel W. I. Crane's handwritten "certificate of marriage of Henry Tolford and Lucy I Blowers," dated December 29, 1852. The document is among the papers Lucy filed with her application for a pension, following her husband's death. (United States Government, National Archives, Washington, D.C.)

7. This physical description of William Henry Tolford is found on his re-enlistment papers filed at Detroit "this 31st day of January 1864 to serve as a Soldier in the Army of the United States of America for the period of THREE YEARS." (United States Government, National Archives, Washington, D.C.)

8. From William Henry Tolford's military records. (United States Government, National Archives, Washington, D.C.)

9. Document No. 191, War Department 1863, attached to William Henry Tolford's re-enlistment papers. (United States Government, National Archives, Washington, D.C.)

10. Collection of Roy K. Blowers.

11. The actual letter from H. Lewis to Lucy, telling her of her husband's death, cannot be located. These, however, are the details that the letter contained, as later referred to in Electa Blowers' letter of May 29, 1864, and in government documents.

12. "The Lieut." is B. E. Westfall, of Henry's regiment. Lieutenant Westfall's family were from Hudson and were friends of the Tolfords and Blowerses.

13. Collection of Roy K. Blowers.

14. Collection of Roy K. Blowers.

15. Randall and Donald, *The Civil War,* p. 419.

16. Smith, *Trial by Fire,* p. 502.

17. "That I well knew the late Lucy I. Tolford, wife of William H. Tolford.... That I was the family physician...& attended her in her last sickness, saw her when she was dying, and after her death.... That I noted her death in my notebook at the time, and have refreshed my memory concerning the same by referring to said note-book this morning." Handwritten document dated June 19, 1871, by "Geo. W. Rice, M.D." (United States Government, National Archives, Washington, D.C.)

IV
Save the Pieces

1. Of course, it is not possible to record the actual conversations that went on while Betsey J. Bills was inscribing the blocks at her aunt's house. Similar topics were most likely discussed, as the information used here was of current interest; it has been gleaned from family genealogies, vital records and census data.

2. Isabel Moore Crosby's obituary states, "She had been a member of the Congregational church 56 years and universally loved and respected." (*Farmer's Cabinet,* March 13, 1885.)

3. Nathan Crosby, *A Crosby Family,* p. 11. Nathan Crosby was a relative of Betsey J. Bills, of the same generation as Betsey's grandparents. His grandfather was our first Josiah.

4. Nathan Crosby, p. 11.

5. Nathan Crosby, p. 10.

6. Fitch Crosby, "Pioneers of Milford."

7. Nathan Crosby, p. 13.

8. Nathan Crosby, p. 13.

9. Secomb, *History of...Amherst,* p. 225.

10. Nathan Crosby, p. 14.

11. Nathan Crosby, p. 16.

12. Nathan Crosby, p. 15.

13. Nathan Crosby, p. 39.

14. Nathan Crosby, p. 16.

15. "Single men were drafted before married men." Also in Charles's favor, "the young men would have volunteered first. People who lived in small towns were very locally oriented. For an eighteen-year-old kid in 1861 who probably did not travel very much, to join the army and see the country was exciting.... After the firing on Fort Sumter, there was a heavy rush of volunteers by May of 1861." (Interview with Dr. James E. Sefton, Professor of History, California State University, Northridge, California, February 1, 1985.)

16. The phrase "He Went About Doing Good" is engraved at the bottom of Betsey's son John H. Patterson's side of the Patterson cemetery monument.

17. From Betsey Bills Patterson's will. (Collection of Ida P. Stow.)

V
A Piece of Ellen's Dress

1. J. W. Reed to Stedman and Arterista Spaulding, from Plymouth, Wisconsin to Ludlow, Vermont, August 17, 1862.

2. Description of Dane County, in the *Wisconsin Gazetteer,* Madison, Wisconsin, 1853.

3. Ellen E. Reed to Stedman and Arterista Spaulding, from Burke, Wisconsin, September 11, 1854.

4. To Leonora Bagley, September 16, 1854.

5. To Arterista Spaulding, October 27, 1854.

6. To Stedman and Arterista Spaulding, September 25, 1855.

7. To Stedman and Arterista Spaulding (continuation of letter begun by J. W. Reed), March 17-19, 1856.

8. To Stedman and Arterista Spaulding, from Glendale Township, Wisconsin, May 13, 1857.

9. To Stedman and Arterista Spaulding, October 25, 1857.

10. Stedman Spaulding to Thomas and Leonora Bagley, from Glendale Township, Wisconsin to Reading, Vermont, July 15, 1858.

11. Joseph and Maria Reed to Stedman and Arterista Spaulding, from Chelmsford, Massachusetts to Ludlow, Vermont, March 21, 1860.

12. Stedman Spaulding to Thomas and Leonora Bagley, from Glendale Township, Wisconsin to Reading, Vermont, August 18, 1858.

VI
Two Pair Quilting Frames

1. *Portrait and Biographical Album,* p. 271.

2. Broadstone, *History of Greene County,* p. 201.

3. Beaver hats with brims, especially broad brims, were commonly worn by Quaker men for the greater part of the nineteenth century. (See Gummere, *The Quaker, passim.*)

4. O'Neall and Chapman, *The Annals of Newberry,* p. 31. This book chronicles Quaker customs in the South Carolina district from which the Evans family moved to Ohio. Their customs would undoubtedly have remained intact in their new Ohio home.

5. Rufus M. Jones, "...A Unique Laboratory Experiment Which Worked," in West, *The Quaker Reader,* p. 405.

6. Jones, in West, p. 405.

7. *Discipline of the Society,* p. 40. This book details Quaker law and custom in the Midwest at the time the Evans family settled there.

8. *Discipline of the Society,* p. 40.

9. Evans, "The Evans Family," p. 23. The Evans family of South Carolina is descended from the same Welsh ancestors as are these distant relatives in Virginia and North Carolina.

10. Helen Thomas Flexner, "Had Jesus What Thee Calls Common Sense, James?," in West, p. 393.

11. Ansley, "Friends."

12. Collection of Elizabeth Josephine Evans Brown, Xenia, Ohio.

13. From the inventory and will of Sarah Evans, Greene County Probate Court, Book G, p. 269.

14. From a telephone conversation with Sarah S. Evans's grandson, Don Scarff Evans of Tampa, Florida, in October 1984.

15. The quotations in this and the next two paragraphs are from Emma Evans's handwritten diary, which she kept during her first term of teaching school, March 29, 1880 ("I commenced my school on the 29, of March 1880, had 12 scholars, oh! how I dreaded it but it was not so bad after all.") to June 9, 1880. Included in her notebook are verses, notes to herself, her school schedule and several pages of solved algebraic problems. (Collection of Elizabeth Josephine Evans Brown, Xenia, Ohio.)

16. First line of verse engraved on Emma Evans's gravestone, Woodland Cemetery, Xenia, Ohio.

17. From verse on Emma Evans's gravestone.

VII
Julia's Legacy

1. From an interview with Esther Wells Bundy, a great-granddaughter of Julia and Orra Crosby, Amherst, New Hampshire, November 15, 1984.

2. All that remains of the village originally called Hardwick is a cluster of eight early clapboard houses, including Colonel Warner's Stage House built in 1799 and the general store erected several years later. This unusual historic site, with the monument to the Bayley-Hazen Road nearby, is a quiet, secluded little community now, its importance and history forgotten by all but a few local residents. Gradually, due to water power on the Lamoille River, business moved southwest, to the village of Lamoilleville, now called Hardwick.

3. From a telephone conversation with Marion Smith Sartelle, on September 16, 1984. Quoted are the phrases she remembers her grandmother Kate Stevens Smith (stepdaughter of Joseph Stevens) using when describing her childhood in the Stevens' home.

4. From records for the "University of Vermont (for use in General Catalogue, 1900)," filled out by Levi Otho Stevens, brother of Julia and Simeon Hadley Stevens. (Collection of Judith Kane, East Hardwick, Vermont.)

5. United States Government, Federal Census Records for 1860, Washington, D.C.; Child, *Gazetteer of Washington County,* p. 219.

6. From an account written by David Tuttle, quoted in Spaulding, "Hardwick Village History."

7. Quoted from a newspaper article by J. A. Kidder, extant in a manuscript copy in the collection of Judith Kane.

8. Hemenway, *The Vermont Historical Gazetteer,* I, 325.

9. Many of the details in the preceding two paragraphs are taken from conversations and correspondence with Sherburne and Seraphine Wiswell's granddaughter Esther Wells Bundy.

10. Hessel, "The Quiet Virtues," p. 265.

VIII
Fannie's Missing Quilt

1. From a letter written to Barbara McGillivray Lewis, signed "Uncle M S Harris Manford." The exact date of the letter is unknown but is estimated to be about 1961 or 1962.

Bibliography

General

Adrosko, Rita J. *Natural Dyes and Home Dyeing*. New York: Dover Publications, Inc., 1971.

Bealer, Alex W., and John O. Ellis. *The Log Cabin: Homes of the American Wilderness*. Barre, Mass.: Barre Publishing, 1978.

Beeson, Paul, and Walsh McDermott, eds. *Cecil-Loeb Textbook of Medicine*. Philadelphia: W. B. Saunders Company, 1975.

Bemiss, Elijah. *The Dyer's Companion*. Reprint of the 1815 edition, with an introduction by Rita J. Adrosko. New York: Dover Publications, Inc., 1973.

Boatner, Mark Mayo. *The Civil War Dictionary*. New York: David McKay Company, Inc., 1959.

Carlisle, Lilian Baker. *Hat Boxes and Bandboxes at Shelburne Museum*, Museum Pamphlet Series, no. 4. Shelburne, Vt., 1960.

Carlisle, Lilian Baker. *Pieced Work & Appliqué Quilts at Shelburne Museum*, Museum Pamphlet Series, no. 2. Shelburne, Vt., 1957.

Coit, Margaret L., ed. *The Sweep Westward*. New York: Time-Life Books, 1963.

Colby, Averil. *Patchwork*. London: B. T. Batsford, Ltd., 1973.

Colby, Averil. *Quilting*. New York: Charles Scribner's Sons, 1972.

Cole, Arthur Charles. *The Irrepressible Conflict, 1850-1865*. New York: The Macmillan Company, 1934.

Cooper, Grace Rogers. *The Copp Family Textiles*. Washington: Smithsonian Institution Press, 1971.

Cunnington, Phillis, and Catherine Lucas. *Costume for Births, Marriages & Deaths*. New York: Barnes & Noble Books, 1972.

Dillmont, Th. de. *The Complete Encyclopedia of Needlework*. Philadelphia: Running Press Inc., 1972.

Dunbar, Seymour. *A History of Travel in America*. New York: Tudor Publishing Company, 1937.

Earle, Alice Morse. *Home Life in Colonial Days*. New York: The Macmillan Company, 1960. Reprint of 1898 edition.

Ehrenreich, Barbara, and Deirdre English. *For Her Own Good*. Garden City, N.Y.: Anchor Press, 1978.

Fennelly, Catherine. *The Garb of Country New Englanders, 1790-1840: Costumes at Old Sturbridge Village*. Sturbridge, Mass.: The Meriden Gravure Company, 1961.

Fennelly, Catherine. *Textiles in New England, 1790-1840*. Sturbridge, Mass.: Old Sturbridge Village, 1961.

Fishbein, Morris, and Justin Fishbein, eds. *Fishbein's Illustrated Medical and Health Encyclopedia*. New York: H. S. Stuttman Co., Inc., 1977.

Frocks and Curls, the Clothing Industry and Women's Fashions from 1850 to 1900 in Hampshire County and Vicinity. Catalogue for an exhibit prepared by Carla Tscherny at Hampshire College, Amherst, Massachusetts, April 25-29, 1978.

Gilbert, George. *Photography: The Early Years*. New York: Harper & Row, 1980.

Hardingham, Martin. *The Fabric Catalog*. New York: Pocket Books, 1978.

Irwin, John, and Katharine B. Brett. *Origins of Chintz*. London: Butler and Tanner, Ltd., 1970.

Katzenberg, Dena S. *Baltimore Album Quilts*. Baltimore: The Baltimore Museum of Art, 1981.

Lord, Priscilla Sawyer, and Daniel J. Foley. *The Folk Arts and Crafts of New England*. Philadelphia: Chilton Book Company, 1965.

Mansfield, David Lufkin. *The History of the Town of Dummerston*. Ludlow, Vt.: Miss A. M. Hemenway, 1884.

Marks, Geoffrey, and William K. Beatty. *Epidemics*. New York: Charles Scribner's Sons, 1976.

McClellan, Elisabeth. *Historic Dress in America, 1800-1870*. Philadelphia: George W. Jacobs & Co., 1910.

McMorris, Penny. *Crazy Quilts*. New York: E. P. Dutton, Inc., 1984.

Montgomery, Florence M. *Printed Textiles: English and American Cottons and Linens 1700-1850*. New York: Viking Press, 1970.

Morris, Richard B., ed. *The Making of a Nation*. New York: Time-Life Books, 1963.

Orlofsky, Patsy, and Myron Orlofsky. *Quilts in America*. New York: McGraw-Hill Book Company, 1974.

Peto, Florence. *American Quilts and Coverlets*. New York: Chanticleer Press, 1949.

Pettit, Florence H. *America's Indigo Blues*. New York: Hastings House, 1974.

Pettit, Florence H. *America's Printed & Painted Fabrics*. New York: Hastings House, 1970.

Randall, James G., and David Donald. *The Civil War and Reconstruction*. Lexington, Mass.: D. C. Heath & Co., 1969.

Riegel, Robert E. *Young America, 1830-1840*. Norman: University of Oklahoma Press, 1949.

Smith, Page. *Trial by Fire: A People's History of the Civil War and Reconstruction*. New York: McGraw-Hill Book Company, 1982.

Van Wagenen, Jared. *The Golden Age of Homespun*. Ithaca, N.Y.: Cornell University Press, 1953.

I
Remember Me

Carvalho, David N. *Forty Centuries of Ink*. New York: Burt Franklin, 1971. Reprint of 1904 original.

Davids, Thaddeus. *The History of Ink, including Its Etymology, Chemistry, and Bibliography*. New York: Thaddeus Davids & Co., [n.d.].

Description des machines et procédés pour lesquels des brevets d'invention ont été pris. Paris: Direction du commerce intérieur et des manufactures, 1839.

Early Unnumbered United States Patents, 1790-1836. Woodbridge, Conn.: Research Publications, Inc., 1980.

Finley, Ruth E. *The Lady of Godey's: Sarah Josepha Hale*. Philadelphia: J. B. Lippincott Company, 1931.

Godey's Lady's Book and Magazine. 1830-1886.

Halacy, Dan. *Census: 190 Years of Counting America*. New York: Elsevier/Nelson Books, 1980.

[Joseph Gillott's Patent Steel Pens — advertisement]. *New York Morning Herald*, July 11, 1839, p. 4.

Kunciov, Robert, ed. *Mr. Godey's Ladies: Being a Mosaic of Fashions & Fancies*. Princeton, N.J.: The Pyne Press, 1971.

Neal, Roy. "A Chronological History of Ink," *American Ink Maker*, XXXVIII, ix (September 1960), 38-41.

Repertory of Patent Inventions. London: Sherwood, Gilbert, & Piper, 1838.

Subject-matter Index of Patents for Inventions 1790-1873 Inclusive. New York: Arno Press, 1976.

United States Patent Office. Patent No. 2,176, 106-20, issued to Thomas J. Spear. Washington, D.C.

II
Betsey! I Wish You a Merry Christmas

Atlas of Windham and Tolland Counties. Surveys by O. W. Gray, Danielson, Conn. Hartford, Conn.: C. G. Keeney, 1869.

Baker, Raymond F. *Andersonville: The Story of a Civil War Prison Camp*. Washington: National Park Service, 1972.

Bayles, Richard M. *History of Windham County, Connecticut*. New York: W. W. Preston & Co., 1889.

Bowen, Clarence Winthrop. *The History of Woodstock, Connecticut: Genealogies of Woodstock Families*. Norwood, Mass.: The Plimpton Press, 1930.

Bowen, Clarence Winthrop. *The History of Woodstock, Connecticut*. Woodstock: The Woodstock Libraries, 1973. Reprint of the 1926 edition.

Browne, George Waldo. *The History of Hillsborough, New Hampshire*. Manchester, N.H.: John B. Clarke Company, 1921-1922.

Chandler, George. *The Chandler Family: The Descendants of William and Annis Chandler*. Worcester, Mass.: Press of Charles Hamilton, 1883.

Conmy, Peter Thomas. *The Beginnings of Oakland, California, A.U.C.* Oakland: Oakland Public Library, 1961.

Croffut, William A., and John M. Morris. *The Military and Civil History of Connecticut During the War of 1861-1865*. New York: Ledyard Bill, 1868.

Hillsboro, New Hampshire, Court of Probate. Administrator's Bond and Petition, Estate of Isabelle M. Crosby, Docket No. 9375.

Hillsboro, New Hampshire, Court of Probate. Inventory and Will of Esther M. Thompson, Docket No. 27013.

History of Bedford, New Hampshire. Concord, N.H.: The Rumford Printing Company, 1903.

May, John. "Diary." Unpublished manuscript. Collection of the American Antiquarian Society, Worcester, Massachusetts.

Putnam, Connecticut, Town Clerk's Office, Will of Sarah S. Wright, March 29, 1875.

Putnam, Connecticut, Town Clerk's Office. Will of Betsey Wright Lee, January 9, 1896.

Ramsdell, George A. *The History of Milford*. Concord, N.H.: The Rumford Press, 1901.

Strock, G. Michael. *Andersonville National Cemetery*. Atlanta: Eastern National Park and Monument Association, 1983.

Tourtellotte, Margaret McClellan. *History of the First Congregational Church, Woodstock, Connecticut*. Danielson, Conn.: Racine Printing, 1976.

United States Government. Federal Census 1850, 1860, 1870 and 1880. Windham County, Woodstock, Thompson and Putnam, Connecticut. Washington, D.C.

United States Government. National Archives and Records Service. Military and pension records for Abner Lee. Washington, D.C.

Weber, David. *Oakland: Hub of the West*. Tulsa, Okla.: Continental Heritage Press, Inc., 1981.

Whitman, Walt. *Complete Prose Works*. New York: Mitchell, Kennerley, 1891.

III
Till Death Do Us Part

Allegan, Van Buren and Kalamazoo Counties, Michigan: Portrait and Biographical Record. Chicago: Chapman Bros., 1892.

Beauchamp, William M. *Past and Present of Syracuse and Onondaga County, New York.* New York: The S. J. Clarke Publishing Co., 1908.

Blowers family, Danbury, Wisconsin. Collection of letters written by Martin Blowers.

Blowers, Roy K. Private papers and detailed family history.

Bruce, Dwight H. *Onondaga's Centennial: Gleanings of a Century,* Vol. I. [Boston]: The Boston History Company, 1896.

Church Records from the Town of Pompey. Transcribed from original records by the D.A.R. of the First Baptist Church, Delphi, New York.

Clark, Joshua V. H. *Onondaga; or Reminiscences of Earlier and Later Times;...and Oswego,* Vol. I. Syracuse: Stoddard and Babcock, 1849.

Comstock, Augustin. "The Town of Fabius," *Yesteryears,* X, xxxix (March 1967), 113-119.

Harger, Norma Calkins. Private papers. Detailed genealogical records.

Mason, W. W. Clayton D. *History of Onondaga County, New York.* Syracuse: D. Mason & Co., 1878.

Pompey: Our Town in Profile. Pompey, N.Y.: Township of Pompey, 1976.

Re-union of the Sons and Daughters of the Old Town of Pompey. Pompey, N.Y.: [n.p.], 1875.

"Town of Pompey." Pompey, N.Y.: Pompey Historical Society, 1982. Unpublished manuscript.

United States Government. Federal Census 1850 and 1860. Onondaga County, Pompey, New York. Washington, D.C.

United States Government. National Archives and Records Service. Military and pension records of William Henry Tolford. Washington, D.C.

IV
Save the Pieces

Crosby, Fitch. "Pioneers of Milford," *Farmer's Cabinet,* June 25, 1894.

["Crosby, Isabel Mooar"—obituary]. *Farmer's Cabinet,* March 13, 1885.

Crosby, Nathan. *A Crosby Family.* Lowell, Mass.: Stone, Huse & Co., 1877.

Milford, New Hampshire, Town Clerk's Office. Death record of Isabel Moore Crosby, Vol. 4, p. 3.

Secomb, Daniel F. *History of the Town of Amherst.* Concord, N.H.: Evans, Sleeper & Woodbury, 1883.

Stow, Ida P. Private papers.

United States Government. Federal Census 1850. Hillsboro County, Milford Township and Amherst Township, New Hampshire. Washington, D.C.

Waite, Otis F. R. *New Hampshire in the Great Rebellion.* Claremont, N.H.: Tracy, Chase & Co., 1870.

V
A Piece of Ellen's Dress

Aldrich, Lewis Cass, and Frank R. Holmes, eds. *History of Windsor County, Vermont.* Syracuse, N.Y.: D. Mason & Co., 1891.

Allen, Wilkes. *The History of Chelmsford.* Somersworth, N.H.: New Hampshire Printers, Inc., 1974. Reprint of 1820 edition.

Ames, Azel. *The Mayflower and Her Log, July 15, 1620–May 6, 1621.* New York: Houghton-Mifflin and Company, 1901.

Ancestral Chronological Record of the William White Family. Concord, N.H.: Republican Press Association, 1895.

Babcock, Robert H. *Diseases of the Lungs.* New York: D. Appleton and Company, 1907.

Bagley, Ernest Griffen, ed. *The Bagley Family, 1066-1958.* Raleigh, N.C.: [n.p.], 1958.

Bicentennial History of Milton. Milton, Wisc.: Milton Bicentennial Committee, 1977.

Chiolino, Barbara. "A Box of Letters Concerning the Vermont Family of Abby Maria Hemenway." Unpublished manuscript, 1978.

Chiolino, Barbara. Private papers, including Ellen Spaulding Reed's and Willard Reed's letters and Stedman Spaulding's ledgers.

Elroy. Bicentennial Committee of Elroy, Wisconsin, 1976.

Harris, Joseph N. *History of Ludlow, Vermont.* Charlestown, N.H.: Ina Harris Harding and Archie Frank Harding, 1949.

History of Dane County, Wisconsin. Chicago: Western Historical Company, 1880.

"History of Juneau County." Unpublished manuscript in the collection of Mauston Library, Mauston, Wisconsin.

Hunt, John Warren. *Wisconsin Gazetteer.* Madison: Beriah Brown, 1853.

Madison, Dane County and Surrounding Towns. Madison, Wisc.: Wm. J. Park & Co., 1877.

McKearin, Helen, and Kenneth M. Wilson. *American Bottles and Flasks and Their Ancestry.* New York: Crown Publishers, Inc., 1978.

Reed, Jacob Whittemore. *History of the Reed Family in Europe and America.* Boston: John Wilson and Son, 1861.

Sherman, May Fowler. "Reminiscences of Elroy, Wisconsin." Read by her, age 81, at a ceremony on December 5, 1944.

Spalding, Samuel J. *Spalding Memorial: A Genealogical History of Edward Spalding, of Massachusetts Bay, and His Descendants.* Boston: Alfred Mudge & Son, 1872.

Statistics of Dane County, Wisconsin with a Sketch of the Settlement, Growth, and Prospects of the Village of Madison. Madison: Carpenter & Tenney, 1852.

Statistics of Dane County, Wisconsin. Madison: Carpenter & Tenney, 1850.

Vital Records of Chelmsford, Massachusetts, to the End of the Year 1849. Salem, Mass.: The Essex Institute, 1914.

VI
Two Pair Quilting Frames

Ansley, Delight. "Friends, The Religious Society of." *Encyclopedia Americana,* 1974.

Broadstone, Michael A. *History of Greene County, Ohio,* Vol. II. Indianapolis: B. F. Bowen & Company, Inc., 1918.

Brown, Elizabeth Josephine Evans. Private papers.

Combination Atlas Map of Greene County, Ohio. Chicago: L. H. Everts & Co., 1874.

Dills, R. S. *History of Greene County.* Dayton, Oh.: Odell & Mayer, 1881.

Discipline of the Society of Friends of Indiana Yearly Meeting. Cincinnati: A. Pugh, 1839.

1855 Atlas from the Map of Greene County, Ohio. Philadelphia: Anthony D. Byles, 1855. Reprinted by the Greene County Historical Society, Xenia, Ohio, 1979.

Evans, Goode. "The Evans Family of Virginia and North Carolina." Unpublished manuscript, Genealogical Collection, Public Library, West Los Angeles, California.

"Friends on the Landscape: A Preliminary Examination of the Society of Friends—Their Settlement and Architecture in Clinton, Highland & Warren Counties, 1795-1860." In the Quaker Collection of the Wilmington College Library, Wilmington, Ohio.

Greene County 1803-1908. Xenia, Oh.: The Aldine Publishing House, 1908.

Greene County Probate Court, Xenia, Ohio. Wills of Robert Evans, Sarah Coppock Evans and Sarah S. Evans.

Gummere, Amelia Mott. *The Quaker; A Study in Costume.* Philadelphia: Ferris & Leach, 1901.

Heiss, Willard C. *Guide to Research in Quaker Records in the Midwest.* Indianapolis: Indiana Quaker Records, 1962.

Hinshaw, William Wade. *Encyclopedia of American Quaker Genealogy.* Ann Arbor, Mich.: Edwards Bros., 1946.

Lucas, Sidney. *The Quaker Story.* New York: Harper & Brothers, 1949.

O'Neall, John Belton, and John A. Chapman. *The Annals of Newberry.* Baltimore: Genealogical Publishing Co., Inc., 1974.

Portrait and Biographical Album of Greene and Clark Counties, Ohio. Chicago: Chapman Bros., 1890.

Robinson, George F. *History of Greene County, Ohio.* Chicago: The S. J. Clarke Publishing Company, 1902.

Trueblood, David Elton. *The People Called Quakers.* New York: Harper & Row, 1966.

United States Government. Federal Census 1850. Greene County, Ohio./Federal Census 1860. Greene County, Spring Valley Township, Ohio./Federal Census 1860. Warren County, Wayne Township, Ohio. Washington, D.C.

West, Jessamyn, ed. *The Quaker Reader.* New York: The Viking Press, 1962.

VII
Julia's Legacy

Child, Hamilton. *Gazetteer of Caledonia and Essex Counties, Vt., 1764-1887.* Syracuse, N.Y.: The Syracuse Journal Company, 1887.

Child, Hamilton. *Gazetteer of Washington County, Vermont, 1783-1889.* Syracuse, N.Y.: The Syracuse Journal Company, 1889.

Davis, Allen. "Hardwick, Vermont, to Clinton, Wisconsin: The Story of Dustin Grow Cheever," *Vermont History,* XXIX, iv (October 1961), 227-233.

Fisher, Sally. "Hardwick Street Once a Commercial Center," *The Hardwick Gazette,* July 10, 1979, p. 1.

Gazetteer of Vermont Heritage. Chester, Vt.: National Survey, 1966.

Goodrich, John E., ed. *Vermont: Rolls of the Soldiers in the Revolutionary War.* Rutland, Vt.: The Tuttle Company, 1904.

Hall, Benjamin Homer. *History of Eastern Vermont.* New York: D. Appleton & Co., 1858.

Hardwick, Vermont, Town Clerk's Office. Birth and marriage records.

Hemenway, Abby Maria, ed. *The Vermont Historical Gazetteer.* Burlington, Vt.: Miss A. M. Hemenway, 1877.

Hessel, Mary Ellen. "The Quiet Virtues of Samuel Chandler Crafts," *Vermont History*, XXX, iv (October 1962), 259-290.

Jeffrey, William H. *Successful Vermonters: A Modern Gazetteer of Caledonia, Essex, and Orleans Counties*. East Burke, Vt.: The Historical Publishing Company, 1904.

Kane, Judith. Private collection of papers including J. A. Kidder's article (footnote 7), Samuel Stevens' property deed, University of Vermont catalogue record (footnote 4).

Pierce, Harvey Cushman. *Seven Pierce Families*. Washington, D.C.: [n.p.], 1936.

Smith, Lewis. Private collection. Letter from Ursula Stevens to Otho Stevens, July 13, 1844.

Spaulding, Anna. "Hardwick Village History." Unpublished manuscript, copy at Jeudevine Memorial Library, Hardwick, Vermont.

United States Government. Federal Census 1800, 1820, 1850, 1860 and 1870. Caledonia County, Hardwick, Vermont. Washington, D.C.

Wells, Frederic P. *History of Newbury, Vermont*. St. Johnsbury, Vt.: The Caledonian Company, 1902.

Wheeler, Edmund. *Croydon, N.H., 1866: Proceedings of the Centennial Celebration*. Claremont, N.H.: Claremont Manufacturing Co., 1867.

VIII
Fannie's Missing Quilt

Arnold, Anna Estelle. *A History of Kansas*. Topeka: The State of Kansas, 1919.

Blackmar, Frank W., ed. *Kansas*, Vol. I. Chicago: Standard Publishing Co., 1912.

Connelley, William E. *A Standard History of Kansas and Kansans*, Vol. IV. Chicago: Lewis Publishing Company, 1918.

Lewis, Barbara McGillivray. Private papers.

Mathews, Milton W., and Lewis A. McLean. *Early History and Pioneers of Champaign County*. Urbana, Ill.: Champaign County Herald, 1886.

Tuttle, Charles R. *A New Centennial History of the State of Kansas*. Madison, Wisc.: Inter-State Book Co., 1876.

United States Government. Federal Census 1870. Putnam County, Indiana./Federal Census 1880. Clinton County, Missouri./Federal Census 1880 and 1900. Champaign County, Illinois. Washington, D.C.

Wilson, Robert R., and Ethel M. Sears. *History of Grant County, Kansas*. Wichita: Wichita Eagle Press, 1950.

Patterns and Instructions for Making Three Heirloom Friendship Quilts

General Instructions

The supplies you'll need: template plastic, ultra-fine permanent pen, rotary cutter with wide plastic ruler and cutting board *or* paper and fabric scissors, artist's soft pencil (white, gray or silver), cotton thread, sewing machine or hand sewing needle, glass-head pins, iron, light-colored towel, pressing surface, batting, quilting thread, needle (Between), quilting hoop or frame, fabric.

1. Choose the pattern you desire to make. Complete yardage and cutting charts are given for three sizes: crib/wall, twin and double/queen. Each pattern includes a diagram indicating the required templates. Use the permanent pen to trace the appropriate templates onto the template plastic. Cut the individual templates apart using either a rotary cutter with a wide plastic ruler and cutting board or paper scissors. Indicate the letter and the direction of the grainline on each template.

2. Refer to the cutting chart for the number of fabric pieces required for each template.

3. Lay each template on the fabric and, using the marking pencil, trace around each template, making sure the grainline on the template corresponds to that of the fabric.

4. Cut out the fabric pieces using either a rotary cutter with a wide plastic ruler and cutting board or fabric scissors.

5. Using either a sewing machine or hand sewing needle, construct the individual blocks according to the sew order diagrams. Use a 1/4″ seam allowance. *Warning:* never stitch into the seam allowances in hand piecing.

6. For best results, it is recommended to press (*not* iron) as you sew. Pad your pressing surface with your light-colored towel. Whenever possible, press the seams in the direction of the darker fabric. After you have sewn a seam, press the fabrics flat to set the stitches in place. Then fold the top piece of fabric back over the stitching line. Press again.

7. Give each complete block a final pressing on its right side.

8. The blocks in each of the three quilts are set on point and joined with sashing strips to form diagonal sets. Blocks are sewn together in diagonal rows with short sashing strips set between each block. The diagonal rows are then sewn together with long sashing strips between them. Be careful to keep the blocks in line when sewing the long sashing strips between rows.

9. Give the quilt top a final pressing on its right side.

10. If the pattern you have chosen requires a quilting design in the sashing or border strips, select one which fits nicely in the space allowed.

11. Use the artist's pencil to lightly mark the quilting design onto the quilt top.

12. Prepare the backing. Cut the selvage edges off the lengths and stitch them together along the longer sides with a 1/4″ seam allowance. Press the seam(s) to one side. Cut the backing fabric to *at least* 2″ larger than the quilt top all the way around.

13. If you will be quilting in a hoop, layer the backing, batting (cut 1/2″ larger than the quilt top all the way around) and the quilt top. Baste the three layers together with a long diagonal basting stitch.

14. Fold the excess 2″ of backing in half and then in half again, bringing the folded edge of the backing to the quilt top. Pin. Hand baste in place all the way around. This will protect the edge of the quilt top.

— or — if you will be using a frame, follow the instructions which accompany your frame.

15. Hand quilt through all three layers following the marked lines or seam lines of the blocks.

16. Bind the quilt. Specific instructions are given with each pattern.

If you are a beginner or are unfamiliar with the basic techniques described above, detailed instructions on cutting, piecing and quilting can be found in *QUILTS! QUILTS!! QUILTS!!!—The Complete Guide to Quiltmaking* by Diana McClun and Laura Nownes, also published by The Quilt Digest Press. This is an excellent resource book for anyone wanting to make an heirloom quilt. It is a worthwhile investment.

Betsey M. Wright Lee's
Friendship Quilt

(shown on page 34)

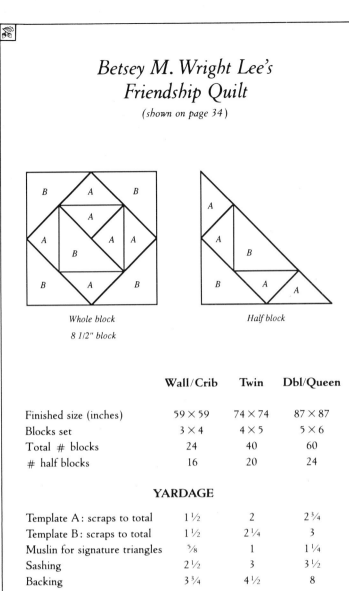

Whole block
8 1/2" block

Half block

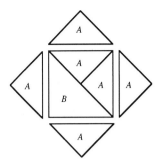

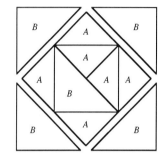

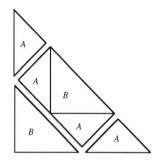

	Wall/Crib	Twin	Dbl/Queen
Finished size (inches)	59 × 59	74 × 74	87 × 87
Blocks set	3 × 4	4 × 5	5 × 6
Total # blocks	24	40	60
# half blocks	16	20	24

YARDAGE

	Wall/Crib	Twin	Dbl/Queen
Template A: scraps to total	1½	2	2¾
Template B: scraps to total	1½	2¼	3
Muslin for signature triangles	⅝	1	1¼
Sashing	2½	3	3½
Backing	3¾	4½	8

CUTTING

	Wall/Crib	Twin	Dbl/Queen
Template A	208	320	456
Template B (print)	112	180	264
(muslin)	40	60	84
Sashing	Cut 2½" wide × length of fabric for all sizes		
Backing: # of lengths	2	2	3

NOTE: This pattern lends itself well to quick-cutting techniques. If you desire to do so, cut the following:

Template A. Cut 3⅞"-wide strips. Then cut to 3⅞" squares. Cut each square in half diagonally.

Template B: Cut 5⅛"-wide strips. Then cut to 5⅛" squares. Cut each square in half diagonally.

CONSTRUCTION

1. Construct the required number of whole and half blocks referring to the sew order diagrams.

2. Sew all the blocks together. Join them to the sashing strips.

3. Prepare the backing fabric.

4. Prepare the quilt top, batting and backing either for quilting in a hoop or a frame.

5. The individual blocks are outline quilted (stitches made *very* close to the seam lines.) Hand quilt through all three layers using small running stitches.

6. Remove the basting stitches from around the edge and the inside of the quilt.

7. Cut the batting and the backing even with the quilt top.

8. This quilt does not have a separate binding. Instead, the edges of the quilt top and the backing are turned in 1/4″ toward the batting layer and machine stitched together all the way around the outer edges.

Lucy Irena Blowers's "Chimney Sweep" Quilt

(shown on page 50)

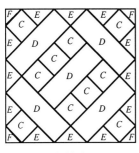

8" block

	Wall/Crib	Twin	Dbl/Queen
Finished size (inches)	39½ × 53½	53½ × 67½	84½ × 84½
Blocks set	3 × 4	4 × 5	6 × 6
Total # blocks	18	32	61
# side triangles	10	14	20

YARDAGE

	Wall/Crib	Twin	Dbl/Queen
Muslin: sashing	1½	2	2¾
side triangles & blocks	1¼	1¼	1½
Print for Templates C and D: scraps to total	1¼	1¾	3¼
Green for leaves	⅜	½	¾
Backing	1⅝	4	5
Binding (straight)	⅜	½	¾
(bias)	¾	1	1¼

CUTTING

Muslin:			
sashing	Cut 2″ wide × length of fabric for all sizes		
Side triangles: # of 14¾″ square pieces	3	4	5
Corner triangles: # of 7½″ square pieces	2	2	2
Template C	36	64	122
Template D	18	32	61
Template E	216	384	732
Template F	72	128	244
Print:			
Template C	144	256	488
Template D	72	128	244
Green:			
Template G (side leaves)	8	11	15
Template H (corner leaves)	8	8	8
Backing: # of lengths	1	2	2

NOTE: *For side triangles, cut each square into quarters diagonally. For corner triangles, cut each square in half diagonally. Cutting triangles in this manner will give you a straight grain of fabric around the entire edge of your quilt top.*

This pattern lends itself well to quick-cutting techniques. If you desire to do so, cut the following:

For Template C: Cut 1⅞″-wide strips. Then cut to 1⅞″ squares.

For Template D: Cut 4¾″-wide strips. Then cut to 1⅞″ × 4¾″ rectangles.

For Template E: Cut 2¼″-wide strips. Then cut to 2¼″ squares. Cut each square in half diagonally.

For Template F: Cut 1⅞″-wide strips. Then cut to 1⅞″ squares. Cut each square in half diagonally.

CONSTRUCTION

1. Construct the required number of blocks referring to the sew order diagram.

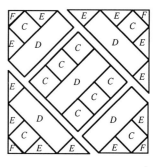

2. Hand appliqué the Template G leaves to the side triangles for three sides of the quilt. Appliqué two Template H leaves to each corner triangle. The paper-basting method of appliqué is recommended.* Trace the outline of the templates onto a sheet of typing paper, one for each piece required. Cut out the paper template patterns and hand baste them to the *wrong* sides of the fabric pieces (which are cut 1/4″ larger than the paper patterns on all sides).

3. Position the leaves onto the appropriate muslin triangles and hand stitch in place.

4. Sew the blocks together in diagonal sets, joining them to the sashing strips.

5. Prepare the backing fabric.

6. Prepare the quilt top, batting and backing either for quilting in a hoop or a frame.

7. Hand quilt through all three layers using small running stitches.

8. The quilt is finished with a narrow 1/4″ binding. Cut strips of fabric 1¾″ wide and sew together end to end to form one continuous strip. With the right side on the outside, fold the strip in half lengthwise and sew to the right-side edge of the quilt with a 1/4″ seam. Turn the binding to the back side of the quilt and hand slip stitch in place.

NOTE: This excellent method is fully demonstrated in QUILTS! QUILTS!! QUILTS!!!—The Complete Guide to Quiltmaking.

Ella-Elizabeth Spaulding's "Album Patch" Quilt made for her by her sister Leonora Spaulding Bagley

(shown on page 72)

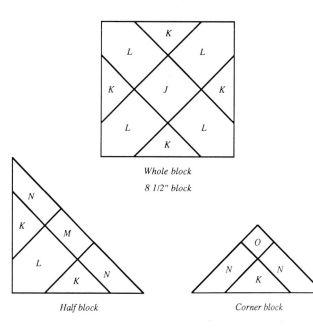

Whole block
8 1/2" block

Half block   *Corner block*

	Wall/Crib	Twin	Dbl/Queen
Finished size (inches)	58 × 62	75 × 79	91 × 96
Blocks set	3 × 3	4 × 4	5 × 5
Total # blocks	15	29	45
# half blocks	11	15	19
# corner blocks	2	2	2

YARDAGE

Muslin:			
sashing & borders	2½	3	3½
Templates J, M & O	⅝	¾	1¼
Template K: scraps to total	¾	1	1¼
Templates L & N: scraps to total	2	3¼	4½
Backing	4	5	8½
Binding (straight)	½	⅝	¾
(bias)	¾	1	1¼

CUTTING

Muslin:			
sashing strips	Cut 3¾" wide × length of fabric for all sizes		
border strips	Cut 4¾" wide × length of fabric for all sizes		
Template J	15	29	45

Template M	11	15	42
Template O	2	2	2
Template K	84	148	220
Template L	60	116	180
Template N	13 + 13R	17 + 17R	21 + 21R
Backing: # of lengths	2	2	3

NOTE: R = reverse template on fabric.

CONSTRUCTION

1. Construct the required number of whole blocks, half blocks and corner blocks referring to the appropriate sew order diagrams.

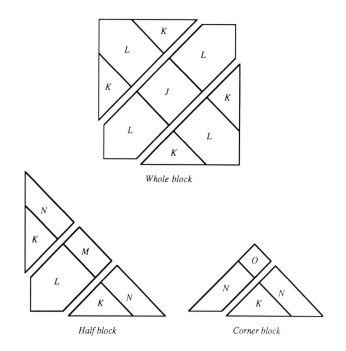

Whole block

Half block   *Corner block*

2. Sew the blocks together in diagonal sets, joining them to the sashing strips.

3. Attach border strips to only three sides of the quilt top.

4. Prepare the backing fabric.

5. Choose a quilting design which fits nicely into the width of the sashing and border strips. Mark the quilting design onto the quilt top. Note that the individual blocks are outline quilted (stitches made *very* close to the seam lines) and do not require marking.

6. Layer and baste the quilt top, batting and backing together with a long diagonal basting stitch.

7. Hand quilt through all three layers following the marked lines or seamed lines.

8. The quilt is finished with a narrow 1/4" binding. Cut strips of fabric 1¾" wide and sew together end to end to form one continuous strip. With the right side on the outside, fold the strip in half lengthwise and sew to the right-side edge of the quilt with a 1/4" seam. Turn the binding to the back side of the quilt and hand slip stitch in place.

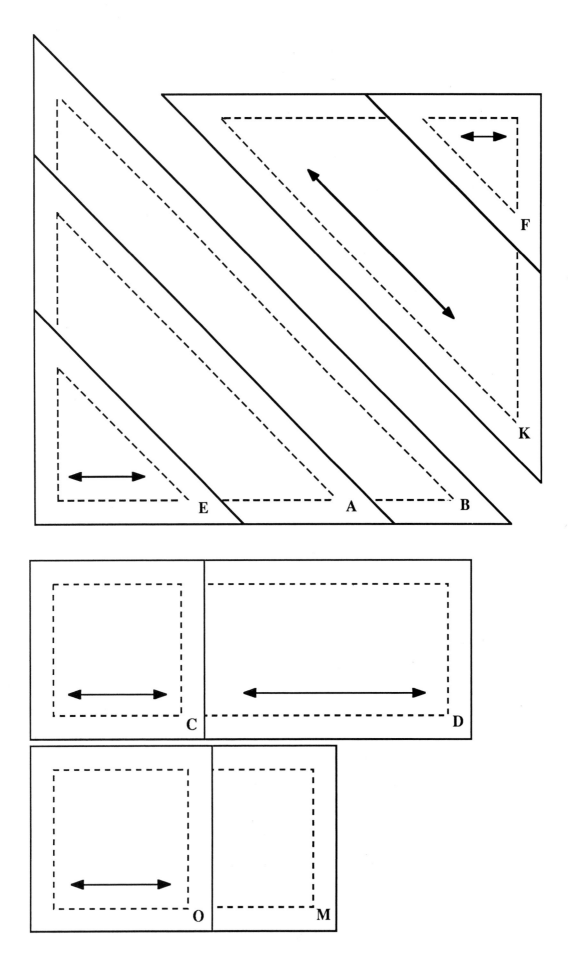